Library of Congress Cataloging-in-Publication Data

Bate, Richard, 1946-
  Soccer speed / Richard Bate, Ian Jeffreys.
    pages cm
  1. Soccer--Training. 2. Soccer--Physiological aspects. I. Jeffreys, Ian. II. Title.
  GV943.9.T7B36 2014
  796.334--dc23

                    2014014398

ISBN: 978-1-4504-2457-8 (print)

The web addresses cited in this text were current as of June 2014, unless otherwise noted.

Acquisitions Editor: Tom Heine; **Developmental Editor:** Laura Pulliam; **Managing Editor:** Elizabeth Evans; **Copyeditor:** Tom Tiller; **Permissions Manager:** Martha Gullo; **Graphic Designers:** Joe Buck and Denise Lowry; **Graphic Artist:** Denise Lowry; **Cover Designer:** Jonathan Kay; **Photograph (cover):** Manuel Blondeau/DPPI/Icon SMI; **Photographs (interior):** © Human Kinetics, unless otherwise noted; **Visual Production Assistant:** Joyce Brumfield; **Photo Production Manager:** Jason Allen; **Art Manager:** Kelly Hendren; **Associate Art Manager:** Alan L. Wilborn; **Illustrations:** © Human Kinetics, unless otherwise noted; **Printer:** United Graphics

We thank the University of South Wales, UK, for assistance in providing the location for the photo shoot for this book.

Human Kinetics books are available at special discounts for bulk purchase. Special editions or book excerpts can also be created to specification. For details, contact the Special Sales Manager at Human Kinetics.

Printed in the United States of America   10 9 8 7 6 5 4 3 2 1

The paper in this book is certified under a sustainable forestry program.

Human Kinetics
Website: www.HumanKinetics.com

United States: Human Kinetics, P.O. Box 5076, Champaign, IL 61825-5076
800-747-4457
e-mail: humank@hkusa.com

Canada: Human Kinetics, 475 Devonshire Road Unit 100, Windsor, ON N8Y 2L5
800-465-7301 (in Canada only)
e-mail: info@hkcanada.com

Europe: Human Kinetics, 107 Bradford Road, Stanningley, Leeds LS28 6AT, United Kingdom
+44 (0) 113 255 5665
e-mail: hk@hkeurope.com

Australia: Human Kinetics, 57A Price Avenue, Lower Mitcham, South Australia 5062
08 8372 0999
e-mail: info@hkaustralia.com

New Zealand: Human Kinetics, P.O. Box 80, Torrens Park, South Australia 5062
0800 222 062
e-mail: info@hknewzealand.com

E5676

SOCCER SPEED

Contents

Part III Tactical Speed

Acknowledgments

During my career, a few significant figures in the profession have had a profound influence on my thinking as a coach.

Allen Wade, former coaching director at the Football Association, was an inspiring man and football teacher and made the game easy to comprehend for an aspiring coach. He instilled in me with the lifelong desire to reach toward his personal and professional standards. Few of his ilk step into a person's life and have such a lasting effect. I will be eternally grateful to him for my attachment to the teaching of the game. Allen was a one-off.

Charles Hughes was a strong influence on my thinking as a coach. Meticulous in both his thoughts about the most efficient way to win football matches and the assured presentation of those ideas, he was an exemplar of coaching and teaching excellence. Controversial at times, he had conviction and clarity to persuade many toward his playing philosophy.

Howard Wilkinson was a strong-willed coach and an adaptable thinker. He knew what it took to win football matches at any level. I have the greatest respect for all that he has accomplished in the game at the professional club level and with the Football Association. Talking with and working with Howard have challenged me to think deeply about the game and to consider what is central and what is peripheral to successful play at the highest levels of the game.

I have worked alongside Jack Detchon, Jimmy Sirrel, Colin Murphy, Graham Turner, Malky Mackay, Sean Dyche, and David Dodds in the professional game at professional club and international youth levels and in coach education. All of these men have indelible personal and professional values. I thank them for their contribution to my life as a man and coach.

Personal friends Steve Rutter, John McDermott, Subramaniam from Malaysia, Chris Ramsey, and John Peacock have loved their involvement in coach education and the wider game. I respect them for their personal and professional commitment and conduct, and I value their contribution to my life and my time in coaching.

In the United States and Canada, Al Albert, Jeff Tipping, Ralph Perez, Tony Diciccio, Ray Reid, Dean Wurzberger, Anson Dorrance, Ray Clark, and Dave Benning have contributed more than they realize to my life. It is a pleasure to know them and call them friends even though we see each other intermittently.

Thanks to all the coaches I have worked with or worked for, whether they are from the professional game or attendees at a coaching seminar, course, or conference. These coaches have challenged me to improve so that I could help others in some small way.

Thanks to Tom Heine and Laura Pulliam at Human Kinetics for helping us to structure this book. Thanks to coauthor Ian Jeffreys for his partnership and renowned expertise in his field of work.

My two sons, Matthew and Nick, have never failed to support me with advice and ideas. They have made me proud and put up with my absences at important times in their lives.

Maggie, my wife, has accepted my way of life, one that has taken me away from her for at least half of our married life. She is the one I depend on and value more than she will ever know or understand. She always has been and always will be the keystone of my life. Time apart has been considerable; time together is so rich. To Maggie I simply say thanks for the support.

—*Dick Bate*

The development of the Gamespeed system has been one of many years of experiment, application, and refinement. My great thanks to all the athletes and coaches (too numerous to name individually) I have had the privilege to work with over the past 5 decades of playing and coaching. You have all left an indelible mark on the system, and your thoughts, support, and patience are appreciated.

My special thanks to three talented young coaches, Sam Huggins, Nick Davies, and Peter Ashcroft. They have been instrumental to the development of the strength and conditioning program at the University of South Wales over the past few years. They have utilized and built on the system and applied it diligently and to great success in a range of settings. Your support and hard work have been invaluable.

To my coauthor, Dick Bate, a man of great integrity and knowledge. It has been my privilege to work with him over the past few years at Cardiff City. His knowledge of soccer and the requirements of the modern game are second to none, and working with him has been a great learning experience. This work has further helped refine and integrate the gamespeed system with the specific skill and tactical requirements of soccer.

To the staff at Human Kinetics, Roger Earle, Tom Heine, and Laura Pulliam. Your help in structuring the work and your diligence in editing the book have been invaluable.

Most important, to my family. To my mother Margaret and late father John who instilled in me a passion for sports and an inquiring mind. This, together with an emphasis on hard work, has been fundamental to my work. To my mother- and father-in-law, Jean and Glenn Jones, who have supported the family during my many coaching adventures—my thanks for your wonderful support.

To my son James. Having the opportunity to coach your son emphasizes the huge role sports can play in a person's development and the critical role of the coach not just in developing performance but also on developing the person. You make me very proud every day.

Last, and most important, to my wife Catherine. A constant source of love and support, she is the foundation stone of my life. I will never be able to thank you enough for the sacrifices you make to enable me to pursue my passion of coaching. Thank you for the most wonderful time together.

—*Ian Jeffreys*

Introduction
A Different Game

Over the course of its history, soccer (both domestic and international) has seen various changes—in the rules of the game, in the footwear, and in the game's organization. But has there ever been a more pronounced era of change than the period from 1992 to the present day? This period has involved considerable changes both in the actual playing of the game and in the surrounding support functions (such as athletic training, sport psychology, sport science, and medicine). Let's take a moment to consider what has changed and why.

For one thing, today's game is quicker. Specifically, both ball speed (as it travels from player to player) and players' own movements are far faster than they were even just 10 or 15 years ago. Players now regularly cover some 8 miles (13 kilometers) per game because they are running faster and moving more often. In addition, playing time has increased by as much as six to eight minutes in recent years. Players now cover distances that are some 50 percent longer than was the case 40 years ago, and high-intensity movements in particular are 50 percent more intense than at the turn of the century. On top of all this, the average time for which players now possess the ball at any given time is just two seconds.

As compared with the game 10 or 15 years ago, today's game also features more—and more accurate—passes as a key element of modern attacking play. More teams now appear to value retaining possession as their attacks develop rather than risking a loss of possession by using direct, injudicious, long (and often hurried) forward-passing styles of play. In addition, though counterattacks have always been a profitable tactic, they are now more prominent, which challenges players to extend their technical skills in order to operate at the higher levels of the game. Overall, then, players are quicker over the ground, the ball travels faster between players, and more teams are making more passes during a game.

More generally, the teams that succeed at the highest levels appear to be moving toward a style of play that requires all players to be efficient, effective, and at times plain outstanding in *any* playing role as they take up unusual positions on the field and are replaced by teammates. For example, central defenders are expected to move forward, both with and without the ball, and to operate in midfield areas just as an experienced midfield player would. Similarly, wide fullbacks are now required to operate as—and therefore possess all the skills of—the "winger" or wide forward. The wide custodians now play *from* rather than *on* the flanks and are just as likely to operate centrally as on the flanks in any phase of play. Midfield players are given the license to break forward up to and beyond the forward players, knowing that the spaces they leave behind will be occupied by others when the need arises. Central midfield players operate more often in unexpected locations on the field and are as likely to take possession of the ball from back players in their own defending third as in the attacking third, as well as on the flanks.

In the bigger picture, team balance and "shape" when a team is attacking are being replaced by ever-moving and interchangeable athletes who can perform effectively wherever they are needed in the team structure. Some might see this lack of a consistent, neat, and balanced team shape as a case of reckless abandon, whereas others view it as exploiting the advantages that can be won by outnumbering and dislocating individual defenders and overall defenses.

With all this in mind, it is perhaps not surprising that the modern game also involves greater variety on defense. In some countries, the major strategy in the past was to press, press, press the ball all over the pitch for 90 minutes, and the majority of teams employed early and high-intensity defending tactics. Today, however, more coaches see the need for a varied approach to defending, and teams are dropping into deeper defending positions before they seriously contest possession. Faced with numerous players who are technically gifted, defenses have learned the folly of merely approaching each opponent in the same way as the last one and using a one-size-fits-all defensive strategy. Instead, both players and coaches have embraced a more selective and intelligent approach in their quest to defend effectively. As a result, both early and later defending strategies are now common at the higher levels of the game.

The typical individual defender has also evolved—into a quicker, more agile, and physically sculpted player who no longer relies merely on the traditional aspects of height, strength, and doggedness in order to succeed. Indeed, the game has moved on. One reason for this change is the fact that players now commonly cross national boundaries. In the English Premier League (EPL), for example, English-born players made 69 percent of all starts in the late 1980s, 38 percent in the 2007–2008 season, and 32 percent in 2012—a radical shift indeed. Though the figures are less dramatic outside of the EPL, the fact remains that the influx of overseas players into the highest-level domestic leagues is changing the style of the game, people's thinking about the game, and the game's very nature.

In many cases, imported players have enriched the skill set at the highest levels of the game—for example, with South American inventiveness, Spanish craft, Scandinavian functionalism, or African freedom—in teams competing in the premier European leagues, where all teams are now blessed with a plethora of international players. As a result, multimillion dollar transfer fees are commonplace, and the world is now the recruiting ground for any player capable of operating at the highest level—whether an experienced player with 70 international caps or a 16-year-old with high aspirations.

Coaching methodology has also progressed, and coaches in the major soccer-playing nations are now required to attend managerial and coaching courses and prove themselves at the highest levels before assuming the title of "coach." Support functions have also advanced remarkably over the past decade, and sport science has become a key part of the modern game. As a result, sport psychologists, match analysts, player and coach mentors, and athletic trainers now take their place alongside mandatory qualified physiotherapists, lifestyle advisors, and medical staff.

With all of these changes taking place, what must coaches be aware of and work toward in order to prepare players and teams to excel in the game's future? Any failure to address this question definitively will leave both the coach and the team ill equipped to compete at the highest levels. For one thing, as the game continues to get quicker, players must not only master the technical basics but also be able to perform them—and respond to others who perform them—at high speed and under severe pressure from opponents. Indeed, only players who possess accurate and "instant" technical and tactical abilities will be effective.

Players must also be able to use unusual and unexpected skills on demand. Indeed, the game is not all about playing at high speed. To the contrary, another key ability—both for individual players and for teams—is that of varying the tempo of play. Those who play one way all the time will find that opponents can become familiar with their tactics and adapt accordingly. Therefore, it is often the *change* of speed that catches players, units, and teams unprepared and unable to cope. This is particularly true of a change from medium- to high-speed play and of rapid directional changes. Changes of speed work best if disguised subtly—but it is often the speed with which the change of speed is made that is vital!

As players continue to perform these technical aspects of the game more and more quickly and also speed up their tactical actions, they must be able to quickly read, recognize, and react to game events as they unfold. This faster style of play demands that players make quicker decisions, take quicker actions, and more quickly change their course of action as needed—including the speed at which they move, both with and without the ball. As a result, success or failure will be determined by small but rapid changes of foot and body position that are required for releasing, receiving, retaining, or running and dribbling with the ball while operating at high speed with high precision. In order to meet these challenges, players must be able to quickly process information, prioritize action, and make (and possibly change) decisions at the last possible split second.

Not only will players' technical, tactical, and cognitive faculties be stretched; in addition, their athletic demands will be increased. Specifically, they must be able to quickly accelerate, decelerate, and perform with the necessary agility and shifts of body weight in order to meet the demand for an all-around quickening in every facet of play.

With this increasingly demanding style of play in mind, this book examines the game skills and requirements that coaches should consider in preparing players to go forward in their playing careers. Not every player will progress to the highest levels. But those who have a chance to do so should practice regularly in both practice and playing environments that challenge and extend their present skill levels. Practice should stretch players beyond their comfort zone—toward the unknown, toward unorthodoxy, and toward unfamiliar solutions to the game's challenges, both as they exist now and as they are likely to evolve in the future.

The book examines present-day game skills and playing circumstances and includes a series of illustrated and detailed practice situations that players and coaches can use as aids to developing the theme being referenced. The book also challenges coaches to think deeply about the skills and tactics that they must understand in order to teach and coach their players to achieve a higher standard of play in the coming years. At the same time, the book is intended for *any* coach, no matter his or her level of involvement. Though much of the detail refers to the game at the higher levels, any coach needs to be familiar with and understand the highest performance levels as a compass for playing the game and helping players develop and enhance their skills and tactical versatility. Of course, any coach works at his or her players' level of understanding and capability, but the coach's thoughts and development strategies are also always led by the requirements of the game and by the challenge of elevating players' horizons—especially for those who have the potential to operate at the highest levels.

More specifically, the book addresses a wide variety of aspects of the game. For example, the technical and tactical parts of the book cover instant passing, play in congested areas, deception, inventive passing, receiving the ball in a variety of circumstances, dribbling and running with the ball, goal scoring, defending skills, and reading the game. The book also examines the necessary athletic qualities for performing at gamespeed and explains the why and how of each athletic aspect. In addition, the book explores the development of different features of speed, along with agility and power, as they relate to the game itself. And once again, the needed athletic qualities are explained in detail.

If players want to possess both the orthodox and the unusual skills required in order to best succeed in the game, they need certain enabling athletic qualities, whether from the domain of speed, power, strength, mobility, or agility. In the final analysis, a player's ultimate success is determined by the combination and harmony of technical ability, decision-making skill, and athletic qualities, along with the psychological facets that are essential both to performance itself and to performance enhancement. These are recognized as the four prime development pillars for developing players.

Key to Diagrams

X   ▲   Attackers/team/players

■   ●   Defenders/team/players

Ⓝ   Neutral player

Ⓣ   Target player

Ⓢ   Sweeper

Ⓦ   Winger

Ⓒ   Coach

GK   Goalkeeper

- - - - ▸   Pass movement

⟶   Player movement

〜▸   Dribble

⚽⚽⚽   Soccer balls

△   Cone

Mannequins

Part I
Physical Speed

Gamespeed: Speed and Agility in Soccer

As outlined in the introduction, the game of soccer is constantly evolving. This changeability places an obligation on coaches to ensure that their players can meet the demands of the modern game in a variety of aspects: technical, tactical, psychological, and physical. In terms of physical requirements, the game is getting faster. For example, statistics from the English Premier League show that players in all positions are covering greater distances, at higher speeds, than ever before. Often, a player performs 50 or more high-speed sprints in a match, and these actions can play a vital role in determining the outcome. As a result, speed is a vital commodity for players who want to maximize their performance.

Speed does not, however, tell the whole story. Players are also required to change direction more than a thousand times per game, or about every six or seven seconds. These directional movements are closely linked with—and in many cases set up—the high-speed actions. This relationship puts a premium on the development not only of speed but also of agility. Therefore, for modern players, speed and agility are two key components that contribute to the ultimate quality of performance they are able to achieve.

These realities of the modern game have led to the introduction of a range of programs intended to help players develop their speed and agility in order to enhance their soccer performance. At this point, however, the effectiveness of these programs is open to debate. What matters in the end is how well these training methods transfer to on-field performance, and thus it is crucial to carefully examine both the exact nature of speed and agility and how exactly they relate to soccer. With that goal in mind, this chapter evaluates the precise needs for speed and agility in soccer, and the remaining chapters outline a system for maximizing soccer speed.

WHAT ARE SPEED AND AGILITY?

Training is a journey, and like any journey it needs an intended destination so that we can plan an effective route for getting there. In other words, before devising a training program, it is essential to understand where we want to go with it. For our purpose in this book, an effective soccer speed program needs to be based on a clear vision of what speed and agility are—and what an athlete can achieve through the training program. Defining this vision, in turn, requires precise definition of the terms *speed* and *agility*—and, equally important, how they apply in the context of soccer.

Speed

In its simplest form, speed can be defined mechanically as distance divided by time. As a basic mechanical construct, it is relatively simple to measure, and it is most commonly measured as the time taken to cover a given distance. In soccer in particular, speed is typically measured by means of linear sprint tests determining the time in which a player can cover distances such as 10, 20, and 30 yards (or meters).

This approach, however, provides only part of the answer when looking at effective soccer speed. Though the fastest person in the world is commonly accepted to be the one who wins the major 100-meter championship in a given year, this ability does not necessarily transfer perfectly into soccer, because the 100-meter sprint is a closed event with little if any variation. For example, the starting mechanisms are exactly the same each time the race is run: the athlete assumes a block start and, when prompted by the firing of the start gun, runs a fixed distance in a predetermined direction along a predetermined path. The winner is decided simply by who crosses the line first. The only external variables are the timing of the gun and the environmental conditions (e.g., wind and temperature).

In soccer, the speed requirements are quite different because the athlete moves in an open environment in which distance, direction, and starting pattern all vary from moment to moment. In addition, the athlete's movements need to be linked with the game's skill requirements. Thus significant differences exist between the speed required for soccer and that practiced by track athletes, and awareness of these differences must guide the way in which soccer players develop their speed.

We also need to differentiate between two important terms related to running speed—*maximum speed* and *acceleration*. Though *speed* is often used as a generic term, these two abilities, despite being related, involve quite separate technical and physical requirements; therefore, an athlete wanting to improve them must use specific training methods.

Maximum Speed

As the term suggests, *maximum speed* refers to the highest speed that a person can achieve. For sprinters, maximum speed is typically achieved somewhere between 50 and 70 meters into the sprint. Although the distance to attain top speed has typically been shown to be shorter for field-based sport players, they still require a relatively large distance (e.g., about 30 yards or meters) to reach maximum speed from a standing start.

Once maximum speed is reached, it is quite difficult to maintain, and, again, it relies on specific physical capabilities (which are discussed in chapter 2). However, given the predominantly short distances sprinted in soccer, typically under about 10 yards (or meters), it is often more important to be capable of achieving a high speed in as short a time as possible—in other words, to accelerate rapidly.

Acceleration

Acceleration is the rate of change of velocity—in other words, how quickly a player can increase his or her speed—and it is a crucial aspect of speed performance in soccer. Again, acceleration requires specific technical and physical preparation, and it needs to be targeted in training if it is to be improved.

This is not to say that maximum speed should be absent from a soccer-specific speed program. In fact, though maximum speed takes a relatively long distance to achieve, the reality is that athletes *approach* maximum speed at a far earlier point in a sprint. For example, in the Beijing Olympics, 100-meter-sprint champion Usain Bolt did not reach maximum speed until 60 meters into the race, but he reached a sizable 73 percent of his maximum velocity at 10 meters, 85 percent at 20 meters, 93 percent at 30 meters, and 96 percent at 40 meters. Therefore, while acceleration should be the major focus of a soccer speed program, given the typically short distances sprinted, maximum speed development needs to play a part, allowing the athlete to accelerate to a potentially higher speed at any given distance.

To add another layer of complexity, neither acceleration nor maximum-speed running happens in isolation. Instead, each is performed in order to accomplish a soccer-specific task, such as shooting, tackling, or passing. As a result, developing players' ability to carry out such tasks effectively while moving at speed should also be an important part of a soccer speed development program.

In addition, acceleration and maximum-speed running are performed in response to the game itself, which may require a player to accelerate in any direction at any given moment. To meet this demand, players must be able to read and react to the game at all times with appropriate levels of speed and control. This requirement for movement quality—not just speed—puts a premium on aspects of performance that have traditionally been associated with the term *agility*.

Agility

Unlike speed, which has a clear mechanical definition, agility is perhaps the most difficult of all fitness variables to define accurately. Even so, we must define it, because it plays a major role in determining one's level of performance in many sports, including soccer. Elite performers consistently demonstrate effective movement capabilities, which enable them to maximize their sport-specific skills and therefore their performance. Indeed, it is common to hear of coaches and commentators extolling the "movement capacities" of certain players, and the single fitness parameter most associated with high-quality movement is agility.

One of the challenges in defining agility lies in the fact that people have often tried to define it as a single capacity. This isolating approach has traditionally involved identifying the main locomotive movements that are common in sports and integrating them into a single definition. These definitions have included major movements such as direction change and velocity change (either acceleration or deceleration).

Sports differ, however, in their movement requirements, and, as a result, an athlete who demonstrates high agility in one context is not necessarily effective in another. For example, how would the movement capacities of the world's top tennis players transfer into soccer and vice versa?

Similarly, any given player's ability level can vary across different movements; for example, a player might have a high capacity for acceleration but a far lower capacity for direction change. For this player, the relative frequency and importance of these movements in the chosen sport would exert a strong effect on his or her effectiveness on the field. For all of these reasons, we can see that the search for a single definition and measure of agility may in itself be flawed.

Another drawback of these traditional definitions is that they analyze agility in isolation. This approach has led to the development of a range of isolated agility tests (for example, the pro-agility test and the Illinois agility test), which assess a player's ability to perform preplanned movements over a predetermined distance and assign a score based on the fastest time. However, though these tests do provide a general assessment of performance in their isolated tasks, they cannot fully assess a player's ability to move effectively in a soccer setting.

In reality, agility is ultimately expressed in a sport-specific setting—in this instance, a soccer game—where agility involves more than just set movement patterns. Yet traditional definitions do not account for the full range of movements deployed in a soccer setting. Nor do they account for the cognitive and perceptual skills required to perform these movements consistently and effectively in a soccer context.

This lack has led people to introduce the concept of reactive agility, which defines agility as "a rapid whole-body movement with change of velocity or direction in response to a stimulus" (Sheppard and Young 2006). Unlike traditional definitions, this definition emphasizes the fact that agility involves responding to a stimulus and therefore also requires cognitive and perceptual skills. At the same time, this definition still suggests that reactive agility is itself a single entity, whereas in fact it is not clear how transferable such abilities and skills are across different sports, or even across the variety of tasks required for effective performance in the single sport of soccer.

Again, then, we face this question: Will the ability to effectively read and react in, say, a tennis context transfer into soccer and vice versa? This lingering question brings up the need to view agility as a sport-specific entity—and, as a result, to the development of the term *gamespeed*.

WHAT IS GAMESPEED?

As mentioned earlier, coaches often comment about a player's quality of movement, and such comments reflect the fact that effective soccer-specific movement involves more than some sort of generic speed and agility. Great players seem to possess an ability to move effectively *on the field* and to link this movement with superior soccer-specific skills. They perform such movement both on and off the ball (indeed, the vast majority of movement in a soccer game is off the ball) and in both offensive and defensive situations.

Although this quality of movement is closely linked to some skills often associated with speed and agility, those skills alone cannot guarantee maximal performance in a soccer game. Indeed, players with superior performance on a closed agility test may not necessarily be able to transfer that performance onto the soccer field. Something more is required, and that something is linked to the context in which players are asked to perform and the task they are requied to carry out. Players' movement on the field of play is intended specifically to maximize their soccer performance, and all actions must ultimately allow them to optimally express the specific soccer skills required in a given situation.

It is here that traditional views of agility and speed can be misleading—and that programs concerned only with maximizing speed and agility in closed situations can come undone. In soccer performance, it is often crucial for players not simply to perform a movement as quickly as possible but instead to control a movement and link it with effective performance of a soccer skill. In this way, agility is ultimately both sport specific and task specific: the player aims to optimize the performance of a task within the overall sport (soccer) context.

This kind of performance requires a different view of speed and agility, which is why I have previously introduced the term *gamespeed* (Jeffreys 2010). This is not merely a simple change of terms. To the contrary, the implications of this change are great in terms of structuring an effective program for developing soccer speed.

Gamespeed is a "context-specific capacity in which an athlete maximizes sport performance by applying sport-specific movement of optimal velocity, precision, efficiency, and control—both in anticipation of, and in response to, the major perceptual stimuli and skill requirements of the game" (Jeffreys 2010). This definition involves a number of key elements that affect the way in which we might construct an effective gamespeed program for soccer.

First, to be effective, speed must be addressed as it is applied *on the soccer field* and within the specific context of the game. Doing so requires that coaches and players carefully analyze the precise requirements for speed within the game itself. The aim of gamespeed is to maximize soccer performance, and thus speed application must ultimately be intricately linked with the tasks that a player performs during the game. It is crucial, then, that techniques developed in the speed and agility program allow a player to optimally carry out soccer-specific tasks.

Again, it is precisely here that many traditional speed and agility programs go wrong, because they focus strictly on techniques that maximize speed of movement rather than looking at the effects of these techniques on a player's ability to actually play the game. To be effective, a gamespeed program must involve thorough analysis of the tasks required of the player, and this analysis must ultimately guide both the overall program and the specific techniques and exercises it involves.

In this way, though maximizing speed of movement is one important element of an overall gamespeed program, it must not be considered the sole determinant of performance. Instead, movement must be carried out at an optimal velocity that allows the player to effectively carry out the given task (e.g., tackling, dribbling, passing). Doing so requires, in turn, that the movement patterns deployed involve precision in their execution in order to optimize the player's control. This kind of skill allows a player to select and apply movement patterns as required in order to carry out required soccer tasks.

Another key element of effective gamespeed is movement efficiency. Because soccer is played over a 90-minute period and requires repeated bursts of movement, players must maximize their efficiency by reducing energy leaks caused by aspects such as inefficient movement patterns, unnecessary muscle tension, or inappropriate compensatory movement patterns. This efficiency enhances players' ability to sustain high-speed and high-quality movements throughout the game.

Yet another critical aspect of gamespeed is its variability. Though speed and agility training is often carried out in closed situations, this approach can never adequately prepare a player for the chaotic and unpredictable nature of a game. In a soccer game, movement is triggered by the action evolving around the player; therefore, it must be applied in relation to the requirements of the game at any given time.

Doing so requires the player to make either an anticipatory response or a reactive response. If these responses are not practiced and developed, the player will always risk being slow to respond to the game and therefore unable to maximize his or her performance, regardless of innate speed capacities. In addition, the player's ability to react and respond depends on being able to assume an effective body position from which to maximize the next movement. All of these abilities, then, must be developed in an effective gamespeed program.

HOW CAN TRAINING PROGRAMS MAXIMIZE SOCCER GAMESPEED?

With this understanding of gamespeed in mind, we can begin considering how to create training programs that help players develop this capacity. To do so, we need to analyze in some detail the following two major areas of soccer play: speed requirements and types of movement.

Identifying the Speed Requirements of Soccer

Speed development in soccer must involve far more than simply following a track athlete's training program; specifically, it must be geared precisely to the requirements of the game. In other words, any soccer gamespeed program must start with the end in mind, which requires carefully analyzing how speed is used specifically in soccer. We can build this analysis around five key questions:

1. What distances does a player typically run?
2. In what direction does a player sprint?
3. How are these high-speed actions linked with movement patterns that come before or after them?
4. What triggers the sprint?
5. What skills need to be incorporated into the movement?

The answers to these questions provide a basis on which we can develop a robust and effective soccer gamespeed program by applying scientific principles of movement.

What distances does a player typically run?

Though the answer to this question varies somewhat by the position played, we can say generally that the typical high-speed movements performed in soccer are short (about 5 to 15 yards or meters). Granted, midfield and wide players (wings and wingbacks) may be required to sprint longer distances, but even these runs are usually fairly short. Overall, then, the relatively short distance of soccer sprints makes it more important for players to develop acceleration capacity than maximum speed. Speed training, in turn, should reflect these distances that a player is likely to run while playing the game. They should also be varied appropriately to ensure that the player develops the ability to be effective over the specific range of distances normally required of his or her position in the course of a game.

In what direction does a player sprint?

Traditional speed training almost always involves starting a sprint to the front, but soccer performance is far more complex. In soccer, a player is just as likely to sprint in other directions—not just straight ahead. As a result, players must develop the ability to start not only straight ahead but also laterally (to the side) and to the rear; this ability is often referred to as multidirectional speed.

However, once the player has made the initial movement, multidirectional sprinting simply involves a standard acceleration pattern. Thus, as discussed in greater detail later in this chapter, the major difference lies in the initiation of the movement. Therefore, speed training needs to be adapted to ensure that a player can initiate movement in the various directions typical of soccer play. To do so, the training program must include exercises that specifically develop these capacities, which means that speed training for soccer must consist of more than sprinting straight ahead.

How are these high-speed actions linked with movement patterns that come before or after them?

Speed in soccer is deployed in the context of the game. More specifically, one feature of soccer is that players are almost constantly in motion; as a result, apart from some dead-ball situations, they seldom apply speed from a standing start. It is vitally important, then, that training reflect this reality of the game by helping players develop the ability to accelerate from a rolling start.

Analysis of the game also reveals that sprints can be initiated from a variety of preceding movements that involve a range of directions—and indeed a range of movement patterns. For example, a player may be moving laterally, using a side-shuffle motion, then be required to sprint forward; alternatively, the player may be moving backward, using a back-pedal motion, then be required to turn and sprint to the rear. Indeed, the number of potential combinations seems endless, and players need to practice these capabilities if they want their speed to transfer to the game itself. Again, these capacities are not addressed in typical track training programs for speed. Therefore, an analysis of movement patterns is provided later in this chapter in order to help develop effective gamespeed sessions for soccer.

We must also take care to analyze subsequent movements. Unlike track sprinting, where acceleration and maximum speed are goals in themselves, these movements are used in soccer to achieve a game-related objective. Therefore, it is crucial that players be able to manipulate their movement patterns to achieve specific soccer objectives. For example, whereas a track athlete would be encouraged to "run tall" during the maximal speed phase of running, this advice is less relevant to a soccer player unless he or she is in clear space and is not required to perform a soccer skill for a period of time. Indeed, even during acceleration and maximum-speed running, soccer players need the ability to adjust their stride patterns to allow them to optimally play the game.

Again, these capacities are never optimally developed by training programs that simply work on track-type speed. As a result, such programs leave players at risk of being unable to adjust their movement patterns to optimize their soccer performance. Instead, soccer speed programs need to focus on the movement combinations and patterns found in soccer.

What triggers the sprint?

Unlike track sprinting, where all movement is performed in response to a starting gun, movement in soccer is perceptually triggered. As a result, players need to learn to react to the game evolving around them, which means that soccer intelligence (covered in chapter 12) is crucial. Typically, a player's movement is triggered by one of three elements:

1. Movement of opposition player(s)
2. Movement of teammate(s)
3. Movement of the ball

Therefore, incorporating these three elements into speed training can help players maximize the transfer between their training and their game performance. This is not to say that one must avoid training involving typical audio cues such as whistle starts. Such training can still play an important part in the development of basic movement capacities. However, coaches and players can also consider how to incorporate other perceptual triggers into training in order to maximize transfer to on-field performance.

When incorporating visual cues, the principle of specificity should take precedence—the closer the cue to the type of trigger seen in the game, the more likely the transfer to in-game performance. Thus, while elements such as flashing lights and colored cones can increase the variability of a drill, they can never ensure maximal transfer because they are not the specific triggers that players face in a game. Examples of perceptually triggered exercises are given in chapter 4.

What skills need to be incorporated into the movement?

This question reminds us of the need to start with the end in mind. When a player performs a speed exercise, he or she should be aware of the context in which the movement will be used in a game. Consider, for example, a change-of-direction drill with a subsequent sprint. By analyzing why this skill is used in actual soccer play—and what soccer skill it is likely to be linked to—we can develop a sequence of appropriate exercises that range from basic movement patterns to exercises that are highly soccer specific. As a result, the basic training work could focus on the technical requirements of direction change, and later applied work could link this movement to the soccer actions of beating an opponent, receiving a pass, and taking a shot on goal. This approach helps a player apply movement patterns developed in training to his or her performance in the game itself.

Classifying Movement

We now have a more precise understanding of the requirements of speed in soccer; however, as we have seen, speed and agility cannot stand as separate entities. Instead, they must be incorporated into an overall understanding of movement that allows us to integrate all of the required movement combinations and soccer-specific skills into an optimally effective program. Programs that fail to address these critical movement links—either by separating speed and agility or by focusing only on linear speed work on one day and only on agility work on another day—cannot maximally develop soccer gamespeed. Effective soccer movement requires the player to develop a range of movement patterns, all of which must be integrated into a gamespeed program.

This is no easy task. The challenge is to break down the complexity of soccer movement into key movement patterns—or, rather, into a classification of all of the movement patterns that a player needs to develop, which can then be progressively integrated into a complete gamespeed program. Here, we can use target classifications that I have previously developed for breaking down soccer movement into component parts that can be developed and integrated into a complete sports speed system (Jeffreys 2010).

Before presenting the classification system, a few points are in order to help us appreciate the value of the system. First, an individual player may need to deploy any of a wide range of movement patterns at any given time, and each of these patterns has a specific objective. In order to help players develop their ability to perform all of these movement patterns, it is crucial that we identify and analyze both the patterns themselves and, crucially, their underlying soccer functions.

In addition, though most speed and agility programs focus on speed of movement, when we analyze individual soccer players' movements we see that speed of movement is often not the prime concern. Instead, the real need often lies in maintaining a position of control from which the player can effectively respond to the game. These movement patterns can be termed transition patterns, and once we identify their function, we radically change our understanding of how to help players develop this type of movement. Transitional movement patterns need to reflect a position of control, and they often differ from patterns deployed when speed of movement is the sole objective. Unfortunately, many traditional speed and agility programs fail to reflect this reality, and as a result they often lead players to develop movement patterns that are actually ineffective in a game situation.

Of course, effective acceleration and (occasionally) maximal speed are critical elements in a game. Indeed, these capacities are highly prized among soccer players and, quite rightly, have been the focus of many development programs for soccer speed. Because the objectives of these movements involve maximal application, they can be referred to as actualization movements, since their overall speed is a crucial determinant. These movements will continue to be an important focus of a soccer speed development program, but they cannot be viewed in isolation.

Earlier, we addressed the concept of multidirectional speed. In reality, multidirectional speed differs from an actualization acceleration pattern only in the earliest stages, in which the movement is initiated. This initial movement depends upon the quality of the player's position and the quality of his or her first movement. Therefore, we need to use a further classification of initiation movements that focuses on the best methods for initiating acceleration. Indeed, a player's effective initiation of movement can be critical in determining the eventual outcome of that particular use of speed.

With these points in mind, we can turn our attention to the target function classifications—transition, initiation, and actualization—which are presented in table 1.1, along with the major target movement patterns for each classification.

Table 1.1 Target Functions and Movements

Transition	• Static—athletic position • Moving—in place, forward, laterally, diagonally, to the rear • Deceleration
Initiation	• Starting—to the front, side, rear • Changing direction—laterally or from a backward direction to a linear sprint
Actualization	• Acceleration • Maximum speed—linear or curved

In this way, all movements can be classified as 1) transition, where an athlete is waiting to react to the game evolving around them; 2) initiation, where an athlete starts or changes the direction of movement; or 3) actualization, where an athlete accelerates. Given that the function of each movement can be identified, a particular strength of the system is that it allows for the identification of the optimal movement patterns with which to achieve the specific aims of the movement. The system enables us to identify the best movement patterns—that is, target movement patterns—for achieving these aims with all movements based on sound mechanical principles. These mechanical principles are crucial because they allow us to develop a technical model for each movement against which to coach and evaluate performance (the optimal movement patterns for each movement are outlined in chapter 3).

As we have discussed, these movements are not performed in isolation within a game, and herein lies the power of the classification system. It allows us to progressively piece together the movements' component parts and, ultimately, combine them with soccer-specific skills to maximally replicate the movement requirements of the game. Chapter 4 outlines methods for piecing together the patterns in order to achieve soccer-based tasks. In the meantime, the remaining sections of this chapter examine each of the target functions in greater detail.

Transition Movements

As highlighted earlier, soccer players spend a large proportion of their time moving while also reading the action unfolding around them—in other words, constantly placing themselves in position to react optimally to the exact requirements placed on them by the game. Therefore, it is essential that they maintain a body position from which they can react appropriately and initiate effective subsequent movements.

This ability to maintain effective posture while moving is key to the concept of a transition movement, and we can understand this reality better in terms of gamespeed than agility. When we frame the discussion in terms of agility, we focus naturally on the performance of movement patterns as quickly as possible without examining how they are used in the sport. This approach fails to fully help us examine transition movements, because they focus not necessarily on speed but on control.

Specifically, transition movements need to be evaluated by how effectively the player maintains control and initiates subsequent movement. When we think about these movements in this context, we see dynamics that differ from traditional agility testing, in which the aim is to undertake a given test as quickly as possible—even if the movement patterns deployed would be relatively ineffective in a game context.

For example, in the T-test—which involves moving laterally, to the rear, and forward—the player's performance is judged solely on the basis of how long it takes him or her to cover a given distance. In reality, however, in soccer, movements such as side-shuffling and backpedaling are predominantly defensive; therefore, the player's aim is to move in relation to the game, while maintaining a position from which to effectively initiate subsequent motion.

Indeed, if the aim were to move laterally as quickly as possible, the most efficient way of doing so would be to turn and sprint in that direction. Thus the T-test is a great example of an agility test that, despite using movement patterns deployed in soccer, ignores the context in which the patterns are used. As a result, in attempting to move quickly, players performing the test normally deploy a technique that is highly inefficient if used in a game.

Theoretically, one might make a transition movement from a static position, in which case the player would need to assume an athletic position but it is far more likely to be initiated from a moving position. The player may be moving laterally (side-shuffling), moving to the rear (backpedaling, backtracking), moving diagonally (doing cross-step running), moving forward, or constantly adjusting position while remaining predominantly in the same place (jockeying). In all of these cases, the aim is stability, and the techniques outlined in chapter 3 enable players to maximize stability and therefore read and react to the game and initiate a subsequent acceleration or soccer skill.

Initiation Movements

Players spend considerable time performing transition movements, but the unfolding of the game inevitably requires them to accelerate in an appropriate direction at an appropriate time in order to achieve a certain goal. This acceleration needs to be initiated effectively by either starting or changing the direction of movement—an initiation movement. Not surprisingly, the quality of the transition movement affects the quality of any initiation and subsequent acceleration, and players who maintain a high-quality transition posture place themselves in the best position from which to accelerate. At the same time, they must also attend to the quality of the initiation movement itself—the first-step quickness that is crucial to effective soccer performance.

Whereas speed development programs have always looked to help players gain an edge by developing an additional "yard of pace," the reality is that players can gain a significant advantage by initiating movement effectively. Essentially, initiation involves one of two main functions—starting acceleration or changing the direction of movement. Starting can be performed in any of an infinite number of directions, but players can give themselves the ability to do so by mastering the ability to start in any of three main directions—to the front, to the side (laterally), and to the rear. Other directions, such as diagonally forward, are basically derivatives or variations of these three main directions.

Though many players are comfortable with the optimal method of starting to the front, in our experience far fewer are good at starting to the side or to the rear, and even then often use flawed techniques. This shortcoming results from the fact that they have not *practiced* using good techniques; indeed, many coaches are unaware of the optimal techniques to use. The good news is that this general lack of proper training gives players a real opportunity to improve their capacities and quickly gain a competitive edge.

In terms of direction change, the most common change in soccer is lateral, or to the side, to one degree or another. Players can improve their ability to change direction in a whole host of lateral directions by developing an effective cut step. In addition, players are occasionally required to change direction, such as from moving in a backward direction to sprinting forward, which requires the ability to plant the foot and perform a subsequent acceleration.

Actualization Movements

After the player has performed the initiation movement, the next phase involves a traditional acceleration pattern. In fact, all accelerations, regardless of their direction, involve an initiation movement followed by an acceleration. The ability to accelerate effectively is crucial to a soccer player and should therefore be a fundamental part of any speed development program.

Several variations come into play. First, depending on how far a player sprints, the acceleration pattern may or may not allow him or her to reach maximum speed. As a result, maximum speed is far more likely to be reached by wingbacks and central midfielders, who cover long distances at high speed, than by defenders and strikers. In addition, high-speed running does not always follow a straight line; therefore, players also need to develop their ability to run a curved pattern while maintaining speed. The optimal techniques for all three of these patterns—acceleration, maximum speed, and curved running—are covered in chapter 3.

Finally, though acceleration is an actualization movement, it may not be the end of the pattern. The player is likely to have to perform a skill at some time during the acceleration and therefore must develop the capacity to adjust their stride and perhaps even decelerate in order to achieve the desired goal. In fact, this capacity is crucial for players who want to effectively perform the technical skills outlined in later chapters.

We have seen that the speed requirements of soccer are quite complex and are intricately related to various on-field realities of playing the game. As a result, a program that simply relies on track-and-field methods or closed agility drills can never enable players to maximally transfer their training performance onto the field of play.

In contrast, a movement program based on the target classifications described in this chapter allows players to develop all of the key movement patterns required during a soccer game. Players can start by mastering these patterns in isolation, then combine them and integrate them with other movements and soccer skills to develop high capacities for soccer gamespeed.

Now that we are equipped with this program outline, our next challenge is to identify the key elements that can limit a player's performance—and the associated capacities that players need to develop in order to optimally develop their gamespeed. Meeting this challenge is the focus of chapter 2.

Factors Affecting Gamespeed

People used to think that running speed was an innate quality that could not be enhanced; luckily, this has turned out not to be the case. Indeed, though any player's maximum speed is genetically limited, it has now been consistently proven that all players can improve their linear running speed. This is good news for players seeking a competitive edge.

In addition, while speed itself can be directly enhanced, our experience shows that players can make even greater gains in the movement-related aspects of soccer. Given the range of movement patterns used in soccer—and the interrelationships between these different movement types—developing the ability to read and react effectively to the game offers players even more powerful opportunities to enhance their gamespeed performance. Unfortunately, these opportunities are rarely taken advantage of in traditional speed training programs. However, having worked with players for many years, we have learned that an effective gamespeed training program can enable players to enhance their movement quality—and, as a result, their gamespeed.

In order to get the most out of any training program, we must identify the key factors that affect performance quality. We can do so by taking what we refer to as a constraints approach to gamespeed where we look closely at the factors that potentially limit performance. This approach gives us an ideal model for examining all of the factors that can influence a player's gamespeed capacity. Specifically, we can identify three broad categories of constraint—organismal, task-based, and environmental—which can be summarized as follows:

1. *Organismal constraints* relate to a given player's unique capacities.
2. *Task-based constraints* are imposed by factors related to the nature of the task, such as the rules of the game and the equipment used.

3. *Environmental constraints*, as the name suggests, are imposed by the environment itself—for example, weather conditions.

ORGANISMAL CONSTRAINTS

The major constraints on gamespeed tend to be individual ones; in other words, they relate to the performance capacities of a given player. With this reality in mind, traditional speed training has focused on physical capacities that fundamentally limit a player's speed potential, especially the ability to produce force within a given time (i.e., the time the player's foot is in contact with the floor).

Indeed, such factors are important, and they do need to be part of any speed development program. But force capacities alone do not determine a player's quality of performance in speed tasks, even in closed situations such as a 100-meter sprint, let alone in an open and chaotic environment such as a soccer game.

Fortunately, shifting from traditional measures of speed and agility to our concept of gamespeed opens up a far wider area of potential constraints for us to address. As a result, we can understand how athletes with different capabilities can all demonstrate effective gamespeed. Indeed, when we factor in the complexity of soccer—in which performance ultimately relies on elements such as situation-specific anticipation, reaction, quality of initial positioning, quality of movement initiation, and subsequent acceleration—we see that traditional physical capacities alone do not determine gamespeed performance. Instead, we need to do a wider analysis, and looking at individual constraints gives us a fuller explanation of the key capacities that a player needs in order to optimize gamespeed performance.

Individual constraints fall into four main categories: perceptual, cognitive, physical, and motor control. Each is discussed in more detail in the following sections.

Perceptual Constraints

Effective soccer gamespeed does not happen in a vacuum; rather, a player uses it to either anticipate or react to a game-specific situation. Therefore, one key to explaining performance is the player's capacity to perceive cues about game action. This may seem like a simple task, but in reality perception is far more complicated than it first appears. In fact, perception is a skill, and the ability to draw key information out of the environment requires deliberate practice.

This is true because, even though the critical information that a player needs to pick out is available within the field of vision, there is also a great deal of "noise" in the playing environment. Noise, in this usage, is the irrelevant information that the player is subjected to in the quest to identify and focus on the relevant information. The player must be able to tolerate and cut through this noise by visually searching the environment for—and then focusing on—the key elements that influence performance. For example, players must identify key aspects of the action, such as opponents' movements, teammates' movements, and the movement of the ball. Over time, through effective and deliberate practice, players can become skilled at identifying and then paying attention to the key elements—and using this information to shape their own responses.

Much of this ability comes from playing the game, and skillful coaching allows the player to more effectively ignore noise and perceive important aspects of the action. A skilled movement coach can also highlight areas of an opponent's movement that indicate the likelihood of various following actions. For example, a player can focus on the types of posture assumed by the opponent, the way in which the opponent positions his or her center of mass, and the opponent's positioning of the feet and hips. Over time, the player can develop the ability to read and anticipate more effectively—but only if he or she is attuned to the correct cues.

Incorporating this type of work into gamespeed training provides an additional tool for making speed training relevant to actual game play. Research suggests that the ability to identify and attend to task-related cues is one reason that elite players produce faster and more accurate movement responses.

Cognitive Constraints

In addition to perceiving important cues in game action, the player must also be able to process the information and use it to guide his or her next movement. To see how these cognitive (thought) processes affect gamespeed, we need to understand how the brain deciphers information and initiates movement. Studies of brain function show that the brain areas responsible for perceiving and processing cues are separate from the areas responsible for controlling movement. Therefore, if a player wants be able to perceive and process key information *and* use it to direct his or her next soccer movement, the player must develop strong links between these separate parts of the brain.

Fortunately, research has shown that we can develop these links by undertaking cognitively challenging tasks that activate both areas of the brain. In contrast, when we do automatic movements, only the brain areas responsible for movement are highly active. Therefore, effective training requires a range of exercises that maximize a player's ability not only to read, react, and move effectively within the game context but also to achieve planned movement or soccer-specific outcomes. If speed is developed only through closed drills that do not develop the needed brain linkages, the player may be limited in his or her ability to move appropriately within the game, especially in situations of high pressure or challenge.

With all of this in mind, an effective gamespeed program must develop the desired brain linkages through progressively challenging exercises that incorporate key aspects of the game. Effective coaching is also crucial in drawing a player's attention to elements of performance that need more work. Specifically, effective questioning can be hugely beneficial in helping a player develop the ability to understand movement.

Physical Constraints

Once a player evaluates the unfolding situation and decides on a movement strategy, he or she is then required to initiate actualization movements (see chapter 1), which require either high-speed running or the performance of soccer-related skills. In soccer, much of this reading and reacting to the game occurs when an athlete is already moving—thus the importance of effective transition movements. The quality of the subsequent initiation movement, and the following acceleration, are dictated to a significant extent by the player's physical capacities, along with his or her technical capabilities (which are discussed in the section on motor control constraints later in this chapter).

One key physical capacity is running speed (in terms of both acceleration and maximal speed), because it is a key actualization movement that offers soccer players significant performance advantages. Therefore, we need to determine what factors contribute to running speed. In simple terms, running speed is the product of stride cadence and stride length. Stride cadence can be thought of as the number of steps a player is able to take each second, whereas stride length is of course the distance covered by the player with each step. Mathematically, if a player improves either cadence or length while the other remains constant, the player necessarily improves his or her running speed. Therefore, a speed training program focusing on actualization movements needs to help the player improve either stride cadence or stride length while also ensuring that the other factor does not diminish.

Because stride length is generally much easier to improve than stride cadence, speed training should focus primarily on enhancing stride length. Problems can arise, however, if one lacks a full understanding of what determines stride length. Specifically, we need to understand the concept of "effective stride length." Stride length is, as the term suggests, the distance covered between each foot fall, but we need to think of *effective* stride length as the distance that the body's center of mass moves with each step. This differentiation may appear trivial, but its effect on performance can be vital.

When players focus on foot placement, they often mistakenly attempt to increase stride length by actively lengthening their stride through extending the lead leg, which places the foot ahead of the body on landing. The problem is that this action applies a significant braking force, increasing the time that the player spends on the ground and reducing stride cadence. In addition, placing the foot too far ahead of the body leaves the body unable to effectively apply force, thus resulting in a less effective push-off. In short, by attempting to artificially increase stride length in this manner, the player is actually more likely to reduce running speed.

In contrast, when we focus on *effective* stride length, these artificial actions at the leg become irrelevant. Instead, effective stride length is increased through propulsive force (that is, propelling or driving force); that is, it is determined by the force that the player is able to put into the ground to actively drive himself or herself forward. In this way, force capacity and running speed are closely linked.

Thus the ability to generate force is crucial to effective speed performance. In fact, this realization ties in with Newton's laws of motion, which state that in order to initiate motion, a force needs to be applied (first law); that subsequent acceleration is directly proportional to the quantity of force applied (second law); and that the exertion of a force in one direction results in an equal reaction in the opposite direction (third law). In other words, to initiate movement, we must apply a force in the direction that is opposite of the intended movement's direction, and the subsequent acceleration will be directly proportional to the amount of force applied.

As these physical realities make clear, no effective speed training program can afford to overlook the development of effective force capacity. Since this book focuses on the technical and applied development of speed, it does not cover force-generating programs, and players eager to maximize their force-producing capacities need to supplement the information provided in this book with an appropriate physical development program.

In order to identify the type of force required for effective speed development, we need to understand what happens on the ground during a sprint. Essentially, ground reaction forces (the force an athlete can apply to the ground when the foot is in contact with the ground) largely determine stride length, since they are responsible for the required propulsive force. Achieving maximal force requires a relatively large amount of time in contact with the ground—up to 0.6 second. However, even when ground contact time is at its greatest—when a player initiates acceleration from a stationary position—the player has only about 0.2 second to apply force.

Therefore, while maximal concentric (muscle-shortening) force capacity is important, it is more important to apply a high degree of force *rapidly*. In fact, as the player accelerates, his or her ground contact time progressively decreases, thus increasing the need to apply force quickly.

In addition, as this movement progresses, the *type* of force required also changes. During a player's initial acceleration, especially from a standing start or at low speed, concentric force is important, since it provides the propulsive force required to accelerate effectively. However, as the player's speed increases, the nature of the force applied varies. Specifically, the player's landing forces increase, and at maximal speed they can be as much as five times his or her body weight.

As a result, the player must first absorb the landing force via a lengthening of the muscle (an eccentric action). This is then followed by a very brief period where force is produced but with no external movement (an isometric action) and then subsequently these forces repel to drive the body forward through a concentric muscle contraction. This cycle of eccentric, isometric, and concentric forces is called the stretch–shortening cycle, and the ability to perform it effectively is crucial to high-speed running, allowing the generation of effective ground forces. Fortunately, players can enhance this capacity through an appropriate plyometric training program.

Clearly, then, what happens when the foot strikes the ground is critical to speed. Essentially, throughout a sprint, a player must constantly overcome gravity. To do so, he or she must exert sufficient force horizontally to drive forward and vertically to attain sufficient height for completing the stride cycle, thus repositioning the opposite leg to be able to produce the next force.

During initial acceleration, ground contact time is sufficiently long to enable the player to generate both horizontal and vertical force. But as speed increases, ground contact time decreases, eventually falling to about 0.1 second at maximal speed. As ground contact time decreases, the player's capacity to exert force also decreases, and so at maximal speed the vast majority of force is directed vertically in order to overcome gravity (at this point, the body already has considerable horizontal momentum). Indeed, it could be that maximal speed occurs when a player is no longer able to generate any additional forces and can therefore no longer accelerate.

Both stride cadence and stride length are closely linked to ground forces. Stride cadence depends on both flight time (the amount of time the athlete is off the ground) and the time spent on the ground. Since flight time does not vary considerably, enhancing stride cadence depends on shortening the time spent on the ground—while still exerting sufficient force to complete a stride cycle and achieve optimal effective stride length. Meanwhile, effective stride length is itself determined by the amount of force produced during that ground contact time and by the subsequent propulsive force. Thus any speed training program must focus on the ability to develop as much force as possible in as short a time as possible by addressing multiple factors, including concentric strength, eccentric strength, rate of force development, and stretch–shortening cycle capabilities.

While force capacity in itself is a crucial element of speed, we must also consider the directional application of this force. A key concept here is that of rotation. If force is directed through the center of mass, any subsequent movement will be in a straight line. However, if force is applied away from a center of mass, the result is a rotational force resulting in a rotational movement. Therefore, in addition to developing their basic force capacities, players must also be able to apply them appropriately in all of the directions required for soccer. Doing so requires players to develop appropriate strength through all parts of the body responsible for controlling rotation and posture.

Finally, in addition to force capacity, effective speed is also affected by two other key physical capacities: stability and mobility. Stability is the ability to maintain alignment and control in both dynamic (moving) and static (still) situations. Mobility, on the other hand, involves the ability to move through a required range of motion both efficiently and effectively.

Gamespeed, of course, is built around movement, and though force capacity is crucial, movement is never optimally efficient or effective without good mobility and stability. As a result, a speed development program should start by establishing appropriate standards of mobility and stability, which, as suggested by Cook (2010), can be assessed effectively through a functional movement screen. In addition, as a player is asked to perform the movement patterns outlined in chapter 3 and 4, care should always be taken to evaluate the quality of his or her technique. Where issues arise, mobility and stability should be checked to ensure that they are not limiting the player's performance.

Motor Control Constraints

A player's capacity to apply force will not transfer maximally to enhanced speed unless he or she harnesses it within movement patterns appropriate to the game. Therefore, speed development programs also need to help players develop their technical capabilities. As with all skills, appropriate technical development for soccer takes considerable time, and where possible it should conform to the generally-accepted principles of skill development.

Essentially, the player needs to build appropriate motor "programs" for all of the movements that he or she will deploy in a soccer game—in effect, a human version of computer software to operate the player's body. As with a computer system, regardless of the quality of the hardware (in this case, the player's body), optimal functioning is possible only with well developed software. This human software for soccer can be developed only through repetition and progression.

To set up effective training, we can turn to the target movement classifications discussed in chapter 1. These classifications form the structure for building the needed motor programs. We also need to understand how the human body builds its motor programs. It does so by developing what are known as schema—broad patterns for any given skill that can then be adapted appropriately. For example, a player can develop a backpedal pattern and, over time, learn to adapt it (in terms of speed, degree of body lean, depth of center of mass, and so on) to any given situation.

The player's ultimate performance quality in a game situation is closely linked to the underpinning quality of the movement pattern. As a result, the player's development of effective basic movement patterns is crucial to his or her development of gamespeed capacity. This is a crucial aspect of the gamespeed system, which develops—for the first time—a set of basic movement patterns that form the cornerstone of a development program for gamespeed skill.

Novice players need to spend considerable time on appropriately developing the basic skills of the gamespeed system, which are covered in chapter 3. These skills then form the basis of the gamespeed capacities that are progressed into the patterns that the player deploys in a game. However, players should continue to hone these basic movement patterns throughout their playing days, until they become totally automatic. This process requires practice that is not only extensive but also deliberate—practice focused on achieving a specific objective for each movement, thus ensuring that all movement capacities are appropriately developed.

Again, the target classification system is crucial because players and coaches can use it to ensure that they are working on all of the required movement patterns. In contrast, many current speed development programs either omit some of these elements or develop them in a way that does not reflect how players use them in a game. As a result, the player either fails to develop the movement pattern or develops motor programs that do not transfer well to the game—thus leaving him or her at risk of making basic movement errors during game performance.

In addition to developing basic movement patterns, appropriate skill development requires players to create linkages between the brain areas responsible for processing information about how the game is unfolding and the brain areas responsible for automation (initiating automatic actions). Creating these brain linkages requires players to perform exercises that simultaneously challenge their cognitive capabilities and their movement qualities. This work requires a task-based approach to speed development (outlined in chapter 4) to supplement work performed in a closed environment.

TASK-BASED CONSTRAINTS

As we have seen, gamespeed is context specific, and of course the ultimate use of gamespeed lies in the performance of the game itself. Therefore, while basic movement exercises will always be a key part of gamespeed programs, they must be supplemented with context-specific exercises that help players develop the necessary brain linkages to apply speed in game play.

As a result, an effective gamespeed training program must also consider the specific task-based constraints of the game. In fact, context-specific exercises need to account for both the tasks that players perform and the rules of the game that affect how players perform those tasks. We can find a good basis for doing so in the earlier discussion in chapter 1 of the typical distances, directions, perceptual triggers, and skill-base requirements of soccer.

For example, when players perform defensive tasks, their movement needs to be judged not only for quality and speed of movement but also for the player's ability to perform an appropriate defensive task (such as a tackle) at a given point during the exercise. At the same time, the exercise must take into account the soccer rules that govern tackling, so that the skills developed by the player during the task reflect the skills required during game play. Attending to such factors helps maximize the player's transfer from training into the game itself.

ENVIRONMENTAL CONSTRAINTS

In order for players to fully transfer performance from training to game play, we must also consider the environment in which the game is played. Though at first glance it may appear that soccer is played within a relatively standard environment, subtle environmental differences can affect gamespeed performance. Granted, these differences are relatively minor when compared with those found in some sports (such as tennis), where the playing surface can drastically affect the game and therefore the techniques required to perform effectively. Even so, they are worthy of consideration, because a player's performance of a movement-based task in soccer can be affected by elements such as the playing dimensions, the playing surface, the temperature, and the weather.

For example, some playing tactics dictate the space available, in which case players need to thoughtfully consider the types of movement they need to deploy. Similarly, the playing surface affects both the speed of ball movement and the quality of footing. As a result, players need to ensure that, wherever possible, their training replicates the environments in which they will play.

We have seen that gamespeed is a complex phenomenon that is not defined by a single capacity alone. Indeed, this is the fascination of the game—optimal gamespeed is developed only when a player optimizes performance against *all* of the constraints. As a result, we often see players who possess outstanding basic speed and perform outstandingly on sprint tests, yet fail to transfer this speed into the game. Instead, they are often beaten to the ball by physically slower players who possess far better cognitive and perceptual abilities to read the game and anticipate what is happening.

Thus we see that simply following a track athlete's program—while it undoubtedly builds basic speed capacity—can never transfer effectively into soccer performance unless it is supplemented by exercises addressing the full range of gamespeed constraints. At the same time, we also see players who possess great ability to read the game, as well as great technical skill, but lack the physical capacity to accelerate and therefore fail to take full advantage of their soccer skills. Ultimately, then, gamespeed programs needs to be individually tailored to address the key weaknesses and strengths of an individual player.

Developing Soccer Gamespeed

Chapter 1 builds a movement syllabus for soccer. Chapter 2 emphasizes that speed depends on technical and physical performance and discusses how players can build these aspects of performance through repeated deliberate practice and targeted physical training. In this light, gamespeed can be considered a physical skill, and players can maximize their development of the skill by applying the key principles of skill development.

One critical element of skill development—and thus of any speed training program—is technical precision. It is not just the exercise itself that counts but also the way in which it is performed. This distinction is critical because even high-quality exercises, if not performed correctly, at best fail to help the player develop effective technique. At worst, they cause the player to develop technique that breaks down in game performance.

Despite the proliferation of speed and agility drills over the last few years, they have often not addressed the technical models that players need to adhere to when carrying out the exercises. As a result, many speed and agility programs are ineffective at helping players develop high-quality movement, because they provide no technical instructions for carrying out the movement. What players need is a technical model attached to all of the movements identified in the target movement classifications addressed in the chapter 1.

To that end, this chapter outlines the key techniques for each target movement pattern. These models of performance can be used to evaluate a player's movement and make appropriate adjustments. This approach also allows for effective evaluation of movement during soccer practices and games, where movement deficiencies and mistakes may become evident—a powerful tool for any coach.

OPTIMAL TECHNIQUES FOR MOVEMENT

In learning optimal techniques for performing the various movements in the target classifications, players need to focus on target mechanics. In other words, effective movement needs to be based on sound mechanical principles. This foundation ensures that the technical model maximizes the player's performance potential.

In building up these mechanical models, we also need to revisit the target functions—that is, exactly what the player is trying to achieve. In initiation and actualization movements, the aim is to maximize speed performance, which (as highlighted in chapter 2) depends largely on the player's ability to produce and direct force. Therefore, technique needs to optimize the player's ability to place his or her body in the best position to produce force and direct it in the appropriate direction. Therefore, this kind of technique must be part of technical models for initiation and actualization movements.

In transition movements, on the other hand, the requirements are quite different. Here, the aim of the movement is to place the body in the optimal position from which to read, react, and perform a subsequent initiation movement. Thus the emphasis is not necessarily on speed but more often on control of the movement. While in transition, the player does not know what will happen next in the game and therefore cannot predict various aspects of subsequent movement, such as the type of movement required, the direction of movement, the timing of movement, and the skills that the player may be required to demonstrate.

Given this reality, the player must be able to maintain a position of stability during the movement—a position from which he or she can optimally apply a subsequent initiation movement. Therefore, even though the ability to perform these movements at speed is preferred, technique must not be developed in a way that compromises control.

What Is the Mechanical Basis of Acceleration?

Again, as highlighted in chapter 2, acceleration is intricately linked with the ability to apply force. Indeed, as Newton's second law dictates, acceleration is directly proportional to the force applied. However, sheer force alone does not totally explain effective acceleration technique. Force also requires an appropriate directional element, which means that good technique allows a player to maximize his or her force potential—and therefore acceleration potential—in a game situation.

In essence, effective acceleration takes place from a point of instability. Whenever a player's center of mass is placed ahead of his or her base of support, the player assumes an acceleration posture in the direction of the mass. Placing the center of mass ahead of the base of support allows the player to apply force down and back into the ground, thus enabling him or her to accelerate in the opposite direction. Indeed, the direction of the player's center of mass at any given moment naturally dictates the direction of his or her subsequent acceleration.

Force applied directly through the center of mass allows the player to maximize straight-line force because all of the force can be used to generate effective acceleration. In contrast, applying force away from the center of mass results in rotation, and the degree of rotation depends on how far from the center of mass the force is applied. Rotation is counterproductive to speed, and where possible, the aim should be to assume a straight-line posture, allowing force to be applied in a straight line during acceleration and maximum-speed running. Maintaining such posture as movement commences and develops requires a player to use considerable strength and stability.

Figure 3.1 shows a model of acceleration running with a degree of body lean and identifies the importance of straight-line forces.

Figure 3.1 Optimal technique for acceleration.

What Is the Mechanical Basis of Maximum Speed?

The major difference between the mechanical requirements of maximum-speed running and those of acceleration involves ground contact time. As highlighted in chapter 2, the player needs to exert high levels of force; however, as the player moves through a sprint and gets progressively faster, ground contact time decreases, until it reaches a minimum as the player reaches his or her maximum speed. During acceleration, ground contact time allows the player to exert force both horizontally and vertically, but at maximum speed, because the body already has a high degree of horizontal momentum, the critical aim of ground force is to overcome gravity, thus allowing the player to take an optimal stride length. As a result, the vast majority of force at maximum speed is exerted vertically. This difference affects the player's posture, which is far more upright during high-speed running. It also affects the need to exert force as rapidly as possible, creating a high degree of dependence on the stretch–shortening cycle (see chapter 2).

Figure 3.2 Optimal technique for maximum-speed running.

Figure 3.2 shows a model of maximum-speed running, in which the posture is more upright, again demonstrating the importance of straight-line forces, and with the point of foot contact just in front of or underneath the center of mass.

What Is the Mechanical Basis of Stability?

Whereas acceleration requires a degree of instability, that type of posture is inefficient for transition movements, in which stability is crucial. Stability relies on the relationship between three main factors: the player's base of support, center of mass, and line of mass.

A soccer player's base of support refers to the area between the player's feet—and in simple terms, the greater the base of support, the more stable the player. Similarly, increasing this area in the direction of any oncoming force increases the stability in that direction. Widening the base of support also increases the player's stability, though beyond a certain optimal point the player's feet will be positioned too widely to effectively apply force, which is of course crucial for initiating any subsequent movement.

Stability also depends upon the height of a player's center of mass. The center of mass refers to the point around which the body's mass is equally distributed. In general, the higher this center is, the less stable the player becomes. As a result, the player can often gain stability by lowering his or her center of mass. As with base of support, however, an optimal point will be reached; in other words, if the player goes too low, his or her force-producing capacities are significantly reduced.

The third factor is known as the line of mass—effectively, the line drawn perpendicularly from the center of mass to the ground. The closer this line is to the middle of the base of support, the more stable the player is.

Again, for transition movements, stability is crucial, because it provides a position from which the player can effectively read and react to the game and perform any required movement or skill. Therefore, players need to develop technique that optimizes stability yet retains their capacity to apply subsequent force for any initiation movements.

DEVELOPING EFFECTIVE TECHNIQUE

Developing good technique in all of the target movements is critical to building a player's capacity for soccer gamespeed. Indeed, it is the foundation upon which all other capacities are built. We can use the target mechanics just discussed in conjunction with the target function of each movement to develop a technical model for each movement in the gamespeed syllabus.

Optimal Technique

Having established the functions of the target movements and laid out the key mechanical principles underpinning these functions, we can develop appropriate technical models for each and every movement in the gamespeed syllabus. For transition movements, these techniques aim to optimize stability and force potential. For initiation and actualization movements, the techniques aim to maximize force generation, force application, and the needed directional elements.

In order to effectively assess and develop technique, we can use the PAL system of analysis—P for posture, A for arm action, and L for leg action. This system, developed by renowned strength and conditioning coach Vern Gambetta (2007), provides an ideal method for identifying and assessing technique. The system allows us to analyze technique and identify areas for correction or development, whether in a soccer match, a soccer skill session, or a speed or agility session. This approach also provides for effective coaching inputs through appropriate corrective instructions or exercises.

Target Function: Initiation

Starting to the Front

Target Movement Pattern

Acceleration step

Key Performance Aims

To enable players to place themselves rapidly into a position from which they can accelerate effectively and efficiently. This ability is fundamental to effective acceleration and therefore crucial to soccer performance.

Key Performance Points

The player places his or her center of mass ahead of the base of support, simultaneously driving the rear leg forward and driving the standing leg powerfully into the ground. The player needs to develop the capability to make this move from both a square and a staggered stance, though adjustment steps during game play mean that the staggered stance is much more common. The look should be that of a forward lean with the whole body, and there should be no breaking at the hips. The step should be powerful and driven to an optimal length.

P The center of mass is ahead of the base of support.
The torso is straight.
The player leans forward with the whole body.
The eyes are kept up so that the player can see the game unfold.

A One arm is driven powerfully forward and up to shoulder height, while the other is driven backward and down so that the hand reaches at least to the hip.
The angle of the backward arm opens as the arm is driven back and down.

L The lead leg is driven powerfully into the ground in a back-and-down action.
The trailing leg is driven powerfully forward and up.
Ground contact is made with the balls of the feet.

Starting Laterally

Target Movement Pattern

Hip turn

Key Performance Aims

To enable players to rapidly assume a position from which they can accelerate effectively and efficiently to the side.

Key Performance Points

The player lifts or pivots on the foot in the direction of movement and opens the hips toward this intended direction. Simultaneously, the body's center of mass shifts over and then in front of the pivot foot, allowing this lead leg to be driven powerfully into the ground. The rear leg is then driven across the body in the direction of movement. The player should look to achieve a straight-line posture as the movement develops.

P The hips open up in the direction of movement.

The torso opens up with the hip action.

The center of mass is moved over and then ahead of the base of support.

The aim is to develop a straight-line posture.

A One arm is driven back and down and the other forward and up; both movements are linked with the movement of the torso.

The arm appears to cross the body as the leg drives across.

L The lead foot lifts or pivots in the direction of movement.

The lead foot is then driven powerfully down and back into the ground.

The rear leg is driven across the body in the direction of movement.

Starting to the Rear

Target Movement Pattern

Drop step

Key Performance Aims

To enable players to place themselves rapidly into a position from which they can accelerate effectively and efficiently to the rear. This ability is fundamental to effective acceleration when a player has to respond to a ball or an opponent coming in behind him or her.

Key Performance Points

The player lifts the foot and performs a short drop step in the direction of movement, opening the hips toward this intended direction. Simultaneously, the body's center of mass shifts initially over and then in front of this pivot foot, thus allowing the lead leg to be driven powerfully into the ground. The rear leg is then driven across the body in the direction of movement. The player should look to achieve a straight-line posture as the movement develops. The player should remain in an athletic position during the movement and should resist the temptation to raise the body.

P The hips open in the direction of movement.

The torso opens up with the hip action.

The center of mass is moved over and then ahead of the base of support.

The aim is to develop a straight-line posture.

A The lead arm is maintained in its initial position to help with balance.

The trail arm is driven powerfully forward and up.

L The lead foot is lifted slightly and then dropped in a relatively short diagonal step.

As the center of mass is brought over the lead leg, this leg is driven powerfully down and backward into the ground.

The trail leg is driven powerfully across the body in a forward-and-up motion.

Lateral Direction Change

Target Movement Pattern

Cut step

Key Performance Aims

To enable players to rapidly and effectively change direction laterally. This ability is fundamental to creating space on offense and to reacting to an opponent's movement on defense.

Variation

The movement varies considerably in relation to both the incoming movement (whether linear or lateral) and the ultimate direction of the outgoing movement. However, the fundamental pattern remains the same. In an offensive situation, the player may need to precede the cut with a feint, in which the body is shifted away from the intended direction of movement prior to an explosive cut in the intended direction.

Key Performance Points

This movement needs to be preceded by a slight deceleration in which the player lowers the center of mass, widens the step, and shortens the stride. Greater incoming speed requires greater prior deceleration. The player places his or her lead leg outside of the base of support—the more lateral the intended movement, the wider the foot placement. The player needs to control the upper-body motion to develop an effective line of force in the direction of movement. This is initiated with a powerful drive of the plant leg and an effective subsequent acceleration step. The acceleration step needs to be powerful and of optimal length because a stride that is too long puts the player in a poor position for a subsequent step.

P The center of mass is lowered prior to the cut.

The center of mass is maintained toward the center of the base of support (apart from which an offensive feint is carried out).

A The arm of the cutting leg is driven forward and up in the direction of movement to help with acceleration.

The opposite arm is driven back and down.

L The foot is planted straight ahead, and the weight is placed predominantly on the balls of the feet. The sharper the cut, the flatter the foot will appear.

The foot is positioned wider than the knee, which in turn is positioned wider than the hip.

The cutting leg is driven powerfully into the ground to exert lateral force.

The opposite leg is driven forward and up in an acceleration pattern.

Changing Direction Back to Front

Target Movement Pattern

Plant step

Key Performance Aims

To enable players to rapidly assume a position from which they can accelerate in a linear direction from a position where they are moving backward effectively and efficiently. This ability is fundamental to playing effective defense when an opponent suddenly stops and then moves forward.

Key Performance Points

The player needs to ensure that any backward movement is kept under control (see the transition section). To stop effectively, the player needs to place his or her foot to the rear and beyond the base of support—ensuring that the center of mass is ahead of the base—and assume an effective acceleration posture. The player then drives both feet powerfully into the ground and transfers the force from the rear leg to the front leg. As the front leg takes over, the rear leg is driven forward and up as in an acceleration pattern.

P   The player maintains the body in an athletic position as it moves to the rear. On the plant, the player shifts the center of mass forward.

The player assumes an acceleration posture with body lean coming through the whole body, starting at the foot.

A   One arm is driven back and down and the other forward and up; both movements are linked with the movement of the torso.

L   The plant foot is placed behind the body, and the weight is distributed on the balls of the foot.

This plant foot is then driven powerfully down and back into the ground.

The lead leg almost simultaneously drives down and back, and it takes the leading role once the plant is complete.

The plant foot is then driven forward and up as in an acceleration pattern.

Target Function: Transition

Maintaining an Effective Static Position
From Which to Read and React to the Game

Target Movement Pattern

Athletic position

Key Performance Aims

To enable players to assume a position of stability from which they can effectively read a game stimulus and move effectively in response. This position essentially forms the basis of all transition movements.

Variation

The athletic position should be thought of as an ever-fluctuating posture in which foot position responds to what is happening in the environment. Similarly, the depth of the overall position depends on how close the athlete is to needing to respond to the game.

Key Performance Points

The player assumes a position of stability by lowering his or her center of mass, widening the base of support, and ensuring that the line of gravity lies in the middle of this base. The player also makes positive angles at the ankles, knees, and hips to allow for subsequent movement in any direction.

P The center of mass is maintained within the base of support.

The center of mass is lowered to an optimal position.

The torso is maintained such that the back is flat and the chest up and out.

A positive angle is maintained at the hip.

A The arms are held in a relaxed position from which the player would naturally play the game.

L Positive angles are assumed at the ankles, knees, and hips.

The base of support is appropriately wide.

Body weight is supported on the balls of the feet.

The feet are constantly adjusted in response to the outside environment and may be square or staggered.

Maintaining an Effective Athletic Position While Remaining in a Relatively Small Area

Target Movement Pattern

Jockeying

Key Performance Aims

To enable players to maintain an effective athletic position in response to the game unfolding around them when they need to remain in a relatively tight space.

Variation

Jockeying should be thought of as an ever-fluctuating athletic position in which foot position responds to what is happening in the environment. In addition, appropriate torso position is maintained to allow for rapid and effective movement as required. Similarly, the depth of the overall position depends on how close the athlete is to needing to respond to the game.

Key Performance Points

The jockeying technique essentially involves a constant adjusting of an effective athletic position. This ongoing adjustment is achieved by remaining on the balls of the feet in a position that is constantly calibrated to the changing environment. Posture is maintained by coordinated movement along with the feet so that the hips always face in the appropriate direction.

P The center of mass is maintained within the base of support.

The torso is maintained such that the back is flat and the chest up and out.

The center of gravity remains low.

A positive angle is maintained at the hips.

The hips are adjusted in relation to foot movement.

A The arms are held in a relaxed position from which the player would naturally play the game.

L Positive angles are assumed at the ankles, knees, and hips.

The base of support is appropriately wide.

Body weight is held on the balls of the feet.

The feet are constantly adjusted in response to the outside environment and should not become planted.

Moving Laterally

Target Movement Pattern

Side shuffling

Key Performance Aims

To enable players to maintain an effective athletic position throughout the side-shuffling action, thus allowing them to respond and move as required.

Variation

The depth of the overall position depends on how close the athlete is to needing to respond to the game. When the player is located away from the action, the side shuffling can be relatively high; however, as the likelihood of having to respond increases, the athlete needs to assume a lower position.

Key Performance Points

An effective athletic position is maintained while moving laterally, so that the player's posture changes very little as he or she moves, and the positive angles are maintained throughout. Movement is initiated by lifting the outside foot and placing it in a wider position while simultaneously driving with the inside leg.

P The center of mass is maintained within the base of support.

The torso is maintained such that the back is flat and the chest up and out.

The center of gravity remains low.

A positive angle is maintained at the hip.

A The arms are held in a relaxed position from which the player would naturally play the game.

L Positive angles are assumed at the ankles, knees, and hips.

The base of support is appropriately wide throughout.

Body weight is held on the balls of the feet.

The outside foot is lifted and placed wider, while the inside leg is driven powerfully down and out.

Moving Linearly to the Rear

Target Movement Pattern

Backpedal

Key Performance Aims

To help players develop the ability to move backward while maintaining an effective athletic position. In reality, this is seldom done for any real distance in a purely backpedaling fashion, but players need to develop the skill because they will need to use it for short distances.

Variation

The depth of the overall position depends on how close the athlete is to needing to respond to the game. When the player is located away from the action, the backpedal can be relatively high; however, as the likelihood of having to respond increases, the athlete needs to assume a lower position.

Key Performance Points

The player moves backward, taking controlled steps and maintaining an athletic position at the torso with positive angles at the ankles, knees, and hips. The center of mass is maintained over the base of support. Thus, the player assumes a generally forward lean, which facilitates subsequent movement. Unlike in a normal athletic position, the player's feet must be slightly narrower during the back-pedal.

P The center of mass is maintained within the base of support.

The torso is maintained such that the back is flat and the chest up and out.

The center of gravity remains low.

A positive angle is maintained at the hips.

A The arms are held in a relaxed position from which the player would naturally play the game or in a running action.

L Positive angles are maintained at the ankles, knees, and hips.

The base of support is narrower but still stable.

Body weight is held on the balls of the feet.

Adjustment Steps to the Rear

Target Movement Pattern

Backtrack

Key Performance Aims

To help players develop the ability to maintain effective athletic positions when moving to the rear and needing to change the direction in which they are facing during the movement.

Variation

The depth of the overall position depends on how close the athlete is to having to respond to the game. When the player is located away from the action, the backtrack can be relatively high; however, as the likelihood of having to respond increases, the athlete needs to assume a lower position.

Key Performance Points

The player moves to the rear by drop-stepping a foot back at a 45-degree angle and carrying out a side-shuffling action. Thus, the movement involves a generally diagonal and rearward pattern. The player achieves subsequent direction changes by means of a drop step. Throughout, the athlete needs to keep the hips low, because raising them limits the effectiveness of the movement.

P The center of mass is maintained within the base of support.

The torso is maintained such that the back is flat and the chest up and out.

The center of gravity remains low.

A positive angle is maintained at the hips.

A The arms are held in a relaxed position from which the player would naturally play the game.

L Positive angles are maintained at the ankles, knees, and hips.

The base of support is wide.

Body weight is held on the balls of the feet, and the athlete moves in a side-shuffle pattern.

Direction changes are initiated with a drop step.

Moving Diagonally

Target Movement Pattern

Cross-step run

Key Performance Aims

To enable players to track an opponent's run without having to completely turn and run with the opponent. This approach allows the tracking player to cover a potential inside movement.

Key Performance Points

This action involves a mix of normal running action and cross stepping. The hips are generally pointed in the direction of movement. The outside leg moves as in normal running action, but the inside leg crosses over to a point at which the foot is placed in line with that of the outside foot. At the same time, the torso is turned to assume a squarer position.

> **P** The center of mass is maintained within the base of support.
>
> The torso is maintained such that the back is flat and the chest up and out.
>
> The center of gravity remains low.
>
> A positive angle is maintained at the hip, which is turned in the direction of movement.
>
> The upper body is turned so that it squarely faces the intended target.
>
> **A** The arms are carried as usual for effective running action.
>
> **L** Positive angles are maintained at the ankles, knees, and hips.
>
> The outside leg carries out a normal running action.
>
> The inside leg performs a cross step, in which the landing foot is placed in line with the outside foot.

Deceleration to the Front

Target Movement Pattern

Deceleration pattern

Key Performance Aims

To help players develop the ability to decelerate, which is crucial to soccer because it places the athlete in a position to carry out effective soccer skills. Deceleration does not necessarily mean coming to a stop; instead, it simply means reducing speed. Quite often, in fact, deceleration is a precursor to a subsequent movement (e.g., a cut) or to the performance of a skill.

Variation

Though players do need to be able to decelerate into a square position, the staggered position is more likely used in soccer because it can help a defender channel a player into a given area. One leg is placed in front of the other, creating a diagonal angle between the athlete and intended stopping position.

Key Performance Points

When decelerating, the player needs to reassume an effective athletic position. To do so, the player needs to shorten the length of the running stride, widen the base of support, and lower the center of mass. If the deceleration needs to be rapid or even extreme, the player may initially need to lean the body weight back slightly for a very short time in order to reduce speed sharply.

P The center of mass is lowered into an effective athletic position and maintained within the base of support.

The torso is maintained such that the back is flat and the chest up and out.

A positive angle is maintained at the hips.

A The arms are carried as usual for running action and are then brought into an effective game position.

L Stride length is shortened.

The base of support is widened.

Body weight should be held on the balls of the feet.

Target Function: Actualization

Acceleration

Target Movement Pattern

Acceleration pattern

Key Performance Aims

To help players develop the ability to accelerate, which is a key element of gamespeed performance. It follows from an effective initiation movement, which in turn depends on an effective transition position. The aim is to achieve the highest possible speed in the shortest possible time.

Variation

Though acceleration appears to be multidirectional, the acceleration pattern is largely the same regardless of the direction of acceleration. The difference lies in the initiation movement that precedes it.

Key Performance Points

The player places his or her center of mass ahead of the base of support and simultaneously drives the rear leg forward while driving the standing leg powerfully into the ground. This leg action should be supplemented by a powerful and full arm drive. The look should be a whole-body forward lean with no breaking at the hips. After a given leg leads, it should then be driven powerfully into the ground with a piston-like action, as if driving the ground away.

P A whole-body lean is initiated from the feet.

The torso is kept straight.

The eyes are kept up so that the player can see the game unfold.

A One arm should be driven powerfully forward and up to shoulder height, while the other arm is driven backward and down so that the hand reaches at least to the hip.

The angle of the backward arm will open.

L   One leg is driven powerfully into the ground in a back-and-down action.

The opposite leg is driven powerfully forward and up.

The driving foot is dorsiflexed as it moves forward.

Maximum-Speed Running

Key Performance Aims

To enable players to achieve as high a maximum speed as possible. Even though maximum speed itself may not be used often in a game, the ability to achieve a higher maximum speed can help players accelerate more effectively.

Key Performance Points

The drive leg is driven forward and up so that it reaches a point almost parallel to the ground. The shin reflexively kicks forward and then needs to be brought back to the ground. Foot contact occurs underneath, or just ahead of, the center of mass. The recovery leg then cycles effectively behind the body to initiate a subsequent leg action.

P   The torso is upright or leaning slightly forward.

Torso rotation needs to be controlled so as not to become excessive.

The eyes should be kept forward.

A   One arm should be driven powerfully forward and up to shoulder height, while the other is driven backward and down so that the hand reaches at least to the hip.

The arm angle remains relatively constant.

L   Foot contact occurs on the balls of the feet and either under or just ahead of the center of mass.

The drive leg is driven forward and up.

The lead foot is dorsiflexed as it drives forward.

The recovery leg rapidly cycles to enable it to carry out another leg cycle.

Running in a Curved Pattern

Target Movement Pattern

Curved-line running

Key Performance Aims

To help players develop the ability to maintain speed while running in a generally curved pattern. This action is very different from a cutting action, wherein the aim is to change direction sharply. Here, the direction change is more subtle, which allows the player to maintain speed.

Key Performance Points

The player implements effective maximum-speed running technique, but the outside foot is placed closer to the center line and lands toward the outside of the foot. From this position, the player initiates a whole-body lean from the ground up to facilitate movement in a curved pattern.

P   The torso is upright and leaning in the direction of movement.

Torso rotation needs to be controlled so as not to be excessive.

The eyes should be kept forward.

A   One arm should be driven powerfully forward and up to shoulder height, while the other is driven backward and down and comes slightly across the body.

Arm angle remains relatively constant.

L   Foot contact occurs on the balls of the feet and either under or just ahead of the center of mass.

Foot contact is made toward the midline of the foot, and contact is made on the outside of the foot.

This foot contact initiates the body lean.

Effective Technique

Developing effective technique for all of the target movements lies at the heart of the gamespeed system. Once players are equipped with effective movement techniques, they can deploy optimal movement patterns throughout a game, which allows them to maximize the quality of their soccer techniques. Therefore, as you read the later chapters addressing various soccer skills, keep in mind the fact that all of these skills are underpinned by fundamental movement patterns. Indeed, a breakdown in skill performance often involves not only the skill itself but also a mistake in the movement pattern deployed at that time. As a result, players who take the time to develop effective movement skills put themselves at a competitive advantage in game performance.

The amount of time spent on basic movement skills in any given training week should depend on the player's level of performance. Novice players likely need to spend considerable time developing the movement patterns, whereas advanced players should probably spend more time applying these movements in game-specific situations.

For initiation and transition movements, there is little benefit in breaking the movements down into smaller components; instead, performance of the whole movement is a critical part of technical development. Actualization movements, however, can be broken down into smaller exercises aimed at developing specific components of the actions and addressing certain deficiencies in technical performance. Here, it is important to consider the research on skill development in order to maximize the player's learning in any given session. Research suggests that learning is maximized when a session includes a degree of variability and an increased cognitive element. Although performance of basic movement patterns is critical to a player's early development of movement skills, it needs to be supplemented by more cognitively challenging and varied tasks as a player progresses. Thus it is crucial for any gamespeed coach to know how exercises can be progressed.

How Are Basic Movements Progressed?

Although the movements outlined in the Target Function section are highlighted in isolation, the reality is that they are seldom, if ever, deployed as a single movement in a soccer game. Instead, they are integrated and combined, much as the individual movements of a dance routine are combined into a whole performance.

Indeed, observation of the game suggests a whole host of methods by which these movements can be deployed. A look at any transition movement, for example, provides a variety of movement combinations that can be developed sequentially. For instance, from a side shuffle, a player may be required to sprint either straight ahead, to the side, or to the rear. Each of these possibilities offers potential movement combination drills, and degrees of freedom can be added to provide increased variability and randomization (see chapter 4). This type of combination can be applied to all movement patterns, resulting in increasingly challenging tasks for each pattern.

Contextualizing the Movement

The movement patterns developed should accurately reflect the way they are deployed in a soccer game. To achieve this goal, soccer-based tasks, (covered in more detail in chapter 4) offer an excellent way to orient gamespeed drills for soccer specificity. These tasks will be intricately linked with the performance of the soccer-related skills outlined in later chapters. In order to perform these movements optimally, players need to be able to maximize their performance in both the movement elements of the task and the soccer-specific elements. Thus the combined knowledge of the soccer coach and the movement coach is critical in enabling a player to maximize his or her performance.

Despite its apparent complexity, soccer movement can be broken down into a number of component parts. These parts provide the basis for the player's effective movement, and developing the ability to perform them with excellent technical proficiency lays the foundation for the player's soccer gamespeed. Each movement has an optimal technique—based on mechanical principles—that needs to be the focus of analysis and coaching.

Equipped with this knowledge of what the movements should look like, we can now shift our focus to designing sessions and programs that enable players to express these capacities in a soccer context. To this end, chapter 4 examines how all of these elements can be effectively combined into a gamespeed system for use by players at all levels of performance.

Designing Gamespeed Training Sessions

We have outlined, in chapters 1 through 3, the target movements that make up overall effective movement in soccer, along with key coaching points for each movement. This chapter builds on that foundation. Specifically, it examines how to optimize speed development programs to help players develop the basic movement capacities and maximize their transfer from training to soccer performance.

ELEMENTS OF A GAMESPEED PROGRAM

As shown in chapter 2, a player who wants to optimize his or her gamespeed potential must handle a large range of potential constraints. Therefore, all gamespeed programs should address three key elements: technical development, physical development, and gamespeed application.

Technical Development

This element of the program helps the player develop effective techniques in all of the gamespeed movements. It requires long and deliberate practice for each movement pattern, and valuable time can be saved by including these movement patterns in warm-ups. An ideal way to do so is provided by the RAMP warm-up system, which is outlined later in the chapter.

For initiation and transition movements, performing the pattern is in itself the main way for players to develop the technique. For actualization movements, pattern performance can often be supplemented with the use of certain drills that help players emphasize specific aspects of performance. For all of the movements, however, the learning potential in merely performing the movements decreases as the player's level of proficiency increases as the level of challenge and hence cognitive involvement progressively decreases For this reason, we need to provide challenges that increase the cognitive complexity of the exercise to ensure that the player can maintain the movement patterns when put under pressure.

Physical Development

As we have seen, movement and force are intricately related. As a result, no player can maximize his or her gamespeed without developing appropriate levels of all of the physical capacities outlined in chapter 2. Players do not have to develop these basic physical capacities through performance in a soccer-specific context. Indeed, it is almost impossible to develop the physical capacities required to optimize speed without using specific training modalities, such as resistance training and plyometrics. The aim here is simply to develop a basic physical capacity—for example, force generation or the stretch–shortening cycle—that the player can then use in soccer performance.

All too often, in attempting to keep training relevant to soccer, coaches and players try to develop these capacities in soccer-specific sessions or soccer-specific contexts. But this approach, however understandable it may seem, will never maximize performance. Therefore, all soccer speed programs need to be supplemented with an appropriate physical development program.

Gamespeed Application

Technical and physical development in themselves cannot maximize gamespeed performance. Instead, these capacities need to be purposefully transferred into game performance, which means that application work is vital. Such work should focus on two key elements: high-quality movement and contextualization.

First, application work should be done in a way that ensures high-quality performance of key movement patterns, such as acceleration and maximum-speed running. It is impossible to maximize these movements unless they are performed in training, and a player's training program should include performing them with high quality on a weekly basis.

Second, the application element needs to contextualize movement; in other words, it should address *how* the movement patterns developed during technical training translate into performance. This goal can be met by using the task-based approach to developing gamespeed that is highlighted later in the chapter.

The proper proportion of these elements—technical, physical, and application oriented—depends on the unique constraints faced by an individual player at any given time. For example, some players have excellent technical development but lack effective physical capacities; for them, physical capacities should be targeted as the main focus of training. Other players have excellent physical and technical capabilities but lack the ability to apply them effectively in a game context; these players need to spend more time on the application aspect of training.

However, though the relative proportion of these elements varies, they must all be addressed in order for the gamespeed program to be effective for any player. Indeed, though clubs often point to speed as a critical component of performance, many actually perform very little high-speed running in a given training week. Application work should be carried out regularly and should be performed at the highest possible level of quality. In this way, speed training should never be confused with endurance training as this precludes the quality of work required to optimally develop running speed.

GAMESPEED EXERCISE PROGRESSION

One drawback of many speed systems lies in the fact that they lack progression and are predominantly closed (preplanned). Though such drills are initially useful in developing movement—and crucial in developing the underpinning capacities for acceleration and speed—their lack of progression causes their effectiveness as skill development tools to decline over time. This decline poses a challenge for many closed drills, since the only real progression in many of them involves an increase in the speed of application. Even so, this type of exercise should play a role in a speed training program, because basic acceleration capacity and maximum-speed capacity are important aspects of gamespeed performance.

As we have seen, however, these capacities alone do not maximize a player's transfer from training to soccer performance. To achieve optimal transfer, all movement needs to occur within the context of the game and include not only the technical and physical aspects of performance but also the perceptual and cognitive aspects. Skill development appears to be maximized when players are challenged cognitively; therefore, wherever possible, players should be provided with increasing challenges, especially as their level of competence increases.

As a result, in developing progressive gamespeed drills and exercises, it is useful to think about the degree of freedom present in an exercise, which refers to the number of variables that a player must consider and control in carrying out an exercise. Exercises exist on a continuum ranging from totally closed (where all movement is preplanned and the player makes no movement decisions) to totally open or random (where the player faces a virtually infinite number of movement decisions and options).

One example at the closed end of the spectrum is the pro-agility drill. Because it is self-started, the player knows exactly when the exercise will begin, and he or she then runs through a predetermined sequence of movements until the exercise is complete. Thus, the exercise includes no variation, and each subsequent attempt follows a predetermined path.

At the open end of the spectrum, we might find a task-based exercise in which, for example, one player is instructed to get free and receive a pass, while the other player is required to cover all potential movements and try to intercept the pass. In this exercise, both players are unable to plan in advance what will happen; instead, they must respond to what is happening around them.

Variation can be added to any exercise in either a temporal (timing-related) manner or a spatial manner. In the pro-agility drill, for example, temporal variation might be added by requiring the player to start the exercise by reacting to a signal. Thus, the exercise would still be predominantly closed, but the temporal element would add a degree of freedom.

The signal might also involve a directional element; for example, the player might be required to respond either to the right or to the left, depending on the nature of the signal. In this case, we have added both a temporal and a spatial degree of freedom to the exercise, thus increasing its complexity and therefore the level of cognitive challenge. Additional degrees of freedom might be added by requiring the player to turn—not at a given point, but at a further signal—which could be given at any point during the exercise. Again, this change would increase the degree of freedom and the cognitive challenge provided for the player.

In this way, even the simplest exercise can be developed and progressed in terms of its complexity. Doing so allows us to build a system by adding progressive degrees of freedom to a movement pattern in order to increase the cognitive challenge to the player—and, ultimately, increase the player's degree of learning from the exercise. The following demonstrates how this approach can be applied to a side-shuffle pattern between two cones:

1. First, the player side-shuffles from cone A to cone B and back to cone A. The initial movement is performed in a closed pattern,

wherein the player simply moves in a predetermined manner over a predetermined distance.

2. Second, the player side-shuffles from cone A toward cone B, then redirects back to cone A following a signal from the coach. Thus this progression adds a temporal pattern by having the player change direction in response to the random signal. This addition forces the player to use an effective side-shuffle action because he or she doesn't know when the trigger will occur and an ineffective side shuffle uses more time when changing direction.

3. Third, the player starts midway between the two cones and side-shuffles in whichever direction the coach points. This progression uses a spatial and a temporal signal. The player side-shuffles in the direction signaled by the coach, who varies the direction randomly throughout the exercise (which typically lasts three to five seconds). The player changes direction when the coach points in a different direction. Again, these additions increase the complexity of the exercise, because the player no longer knows either the direction in which he or she will move or the time at which he or she will need to change direction. Thus these additions further challenge the player's quality of movement.

4. And finally, two players start midway between the two cones, facing each other. One takes a lead role and the other a following role. The lead player attempts to lose the following player through effective use of side shuffling and cut action. This progression adds a further degree of challenge as the defensive player must read and respond to the movements of the attacking player, who in his or her own right tries to use change of pace and direction to lose the defensive player. Thus the exercise moves toward the types of skill required in a soccer game, and the drill can be even further developed into a specific soccer task by adding a soccer skill and increasing the available movement options.

Throughout these exercises, progression can be achieved by using a range of signals and triggers, which ultimately should replicate the signals and perceptual triggers to which the player will need to respond in game action. Such realism allows training to address the specific perceptual and cognitive constraints of soccer play, and it can be achieved by using effective task-based exercises.

By varying the degree of freedom, we can develop challenges for all movements included in the target movement classifications. This approach lets us build a continuum that ranges from closed to open for all movements and that increasingly reflects soccer-specific gamespeed.

TASK-BASED EXERCISES
TO MAXIMIZE GAME PERFORMANCE

In the end, of course, the whole aim of a gamespeed program is to improve the player's soccer performance, which puts a premium on maximizing the transfer from training to performance. To achieve this goal, we must remember the following fact: although effective gamespeed hinges on underlying physical capacities—and players who possess a high capacity for acceleration and for maximum speed hold a huge advantage over players who do not—these capacities alone do not totally predict gamespeed performance. Rather, they must be used optimally in order to achieve soccer-specific tasks.

We can divide soccer-specific tasks into two main classifications—offensive and defensive—and for each we must also identify the key indicators of successful performance. Offensive gamespeed tasks mainly involve creating and moving into space. These movements can be made on the ball but are predominately made off the ball. As a result, players generally succeed in these tasks when they create separation between themselves and their opponents. Doing so often requires a premovement aimed at getting a defender out of position. Therefore, players who want good offensive gamespeed need to develop not only high-quality movement patterns but also decoy movements or feints.

The aim here is to convince the defensive player that the offensive player is going to move in a certain direction, or at a certain speed, before changing that direction or speed. Players can develop these offensive skills by combining task-based drills with a good understanding of movement. Offensive players who understand what effective acceleration looks like can replicate that pattern in a decoy movement before switching patterns. Performing effective feints and decoy movements requires high levels of movement control, strength, and stability in order to shift body weight rapidly.

Defensive tasks, on the other hand, mainly involve closing down and preventing an opponent from performing a soccer-specific task. Therefore, defensive success is dictated by how well the player reads and responds to the attacker's movements while staying sufficiently close to the attacker to perform an interception, tackle, or other effective action. In doing so, the quality of the defensive player's transition movements is crucial, because the player's ability to initiate effective subsequent movement depends on holding a high-quality position. Players who are forced out of effective transition movements are far more liable to be beaten by an opponent. Clearly, then, the defensive player must not only develop effective movement patterns but also be able to deploy them effectively in the game context. This goal can be met by using soccer-specific tasks in training.

While it would seem logical in training for offensive players to carry out predominantly offensive tasks and defensive players to carry out predominantly defensive tasks, there are in fact many advantages to mixing them up. For one thing, many players need to perform both offensive and defensive tasks during a game; therefore, enhancing the quality of each aspect can be a great asset to the player's overall performance. In addition, offensive players who undertake defensive tasks in practice can better understand the kinds of movement that challenge defensive players and then integrate them into their offensive toolbox. Similarly, defensive players who carry out offensive tasks in practice can better understand what an offensive player is trying to do and then use this perspective to enhance their defensive capacities.

Thus we are equipped with an understanding of what offensive and defensive players are trying to achieve. We can add to this perspective our knowledge of any task-based constraints within the game (such as tackling and offside rules). And we can now construct specific tasks that build on the basic movement patterns to provide a practice context that maximizes the player's transfer into soccer performance. Toward that end, I have identified the following task-based approach that outlines a thought process for developing appropriate tasks:

1. Identify a soccer-related task.
2. Identify the key indicators of performance for that task.
3. Identify any key soccer-related constraints that need to be considered.
4. Identify the key perceptual triggers that affect the task.
5. Design an appropriate exercise.

As an example, consider an exercise where a striker creates space to attack a cross. The following shows the thought process for developing this exercise using the model set forth in Jeffreys' task-based approach.

1. Create space from which to attack a near- or far-post cross.
2. Move defenders away from the space and then accelerate into it.
3. Observe the offside rule as well as rules concerning physical contact.
4. Be aware of movement of defenders and location and movement of the ball
5. An attacking player stands on the edge of the box, just in front of a defender, while a teammate stands 10 yards (or meters) in from

the touchline parallel to the penalty box. The attacking player tries to move the defender away from the space that he or she wants to attack before accelerating into the space to receive the ball.

ENSURING HIGH-QUALITY GAMESPEED SESSIONS

Any gamespeed session needs to involve work of both high quality and high intensity. Because players cannot do high-quality speed work when they are fatigued, all gamespeed work should be done near the start of a practice session after an effective warm-up. In fact, the RAMP-based warm-up protocol allows the warm-up itself to become a gamespeed session. The acronym RAMP stands for the following sequence: raise, activate and mobilize, and potentiate. The RAMP warm-up system was developed to maximize warm-up effectiveness as both preparation for subsequent performance and as a performance in itself. It includes three basic phases, which are outlined in the following sections.

Raise (R)

This phase uses the target movement patterns to raise overall body temperature in preparation for subsequent higher-intensity work. Various patterns of movement can be developed, all targeted to the movement patterns identified in the gamespeed syllabus. The player initially performs these movements in closed situations, starting at lower intensity and building throughout the period. It is crucial for the player to use movement patterns that demonstrate high-quality technique. Indeed, it is often in the initial patterns that carelessness and lack of attention result in poor movement application.

These movements can be developed in isolation or combined into patterns. Either way, using the target movements as the basis for the raising (R) element of the warm-up allows the player to spend considerable time developing his or her movement capacities without any significant increase in overall training time. Here are a few examples.

PATTERN A

In this movement pattern, start at cone A, facing cone B. Run to cone B and decelerate just prior to reaching cone B. Then side-shuffle to cone C, perform a cut step to stop lateral momentum and the backpedal to cone D, perform a plant-step to stop backward momentum, and side-shuffle to cone A. Repeat the sequence in the opposite direction.

PATTERN B

Start at cone A, facing cone D. From there, hip-turn and run to cone B and decelerate, then cross-step-run to cone C before backtracking to cone D, plant-step to stop backward momentum, and cross-step-run to cone A. Repeat the sequence facing in the opposite direction at the start so that the hip turn is worked in the opposite direction.

PATTERN C

Start at cone A, facing cone B. Run to cone B and decelerate, side-shuffle to the outside of cone C, plant the outside foot in a cutstep and then drop-step and accelerate to cone D.

Activate and Mobilize (A and M)

This element of the RAMP warm-up builds mobility in key movement functions and activates key muscles involved in the later higher-intensity work. Exercises can be selected to target any deficiencies highlighted in the functional movement screen and to develop key movement abilities closely associated with gamespeed, such as knee flexion and hip extension. Here are some examples of RAMP warm-up protocols for activation and mobilization that address all of the major joints. All exercises are performed between two cones 10 meters apart.

CALF WALK WITH SHOULDER ROTATION

Walk between the cones, landing on the heel *(a)*, rolling forward on the foot, and rising high on the toes with each step. Simultaneously squeeze the shoulder blades together and circle the arms so that they reach as high as possible *(b)* before being brought through to the front.

INCHWORM WITH ROTATION

Start in a push-up position *(a)*, then, keeping the legs straight, creep the feet progressively to be as near to the hands as possible *(b)*. Then creep the hands out so that the body is in the starting (push-up) position. Next, rotate the body so that the torso moves to a point where it is perpendicular to the floor *(c)*.

HIP FLEXION AND LUNGE
WITH FRONTAL ROTATION

In an upright stance with hands overhead, flex one hip to 90 degrees while maintaining hip alignment *(a)*. Next, drop into a lunge, keeping the torso in an upright position.

Then rotate in the frontal plane so that the hand opposite the lead leg is overhead *(b)*. Finally, push upright and repeat on the opposite leg.

LATERAL LUNGE

Stand facing in the direction of movement and take a long lateral step *(a)*, straightening the back leg and pushing the body weight down and back *(b)*. Repeat to the farthest cone, then return facing the same way so that the other leg is worked.

SQUAT

Stand facing in the direction of movement. Take a lateral step and drop into a full squat position, then come upright and drop-step to face the opposite direction. Repeat for the given distance.

Potentiate (P)

This phase involves a progression to high-intensity work and thus ensures that every session involves a period of high-quality speed application, which is crucial for effective gamespeed development. It also ensures that players are prepared for any subsequent activity that they may have to undertake. Again, rather than being merely a warm-up, this phase can be a session in itself, in which potentiation work focuses on a key aspect of performance.

For example, one warm-up could focus on linear acceleration from a rolling start, another could focus on jockeying and covering offensive movements, and yet another could focus on direction change and subsequent acceleration. In this way, players can develop all key movement patterns and apply them in a soccer-specific context.

This potentiation phase should include the following key elements:

1. The first element should be a *progressive development* of the technical pattern itself. For example, a session addressing linear acceleration from a rolling start should include progressive-intensity sprints from a range of rolling starts.

2. This approach can be followed by an *increase in degree of freedom*. For example, the rolling starts could be initiated on a random signal.

3. The next step should be an *applied element*, in which the skill is increasingly challenged and brought into a more soccer-related context. The rolling starts, for example, could progress to the point where the sprint is initiated with a soccer-specific stimulus. One possibility would be to have two players undertake a rolling start, after which one initiates the subsequent sprint while the other reacts to and covers that sprint. On the next attempt, the players switch roles.

This type of phasing outline can be set up for all gamespeed movements. Here are some additional examples presenting potentiation phases aimed at rolling starts, jockeying, acceleration, and changing direction.

Rolling Starts

PROGRESSIVE RUNS

Run at moderate speed from cone A to cone B; from cone B, accelerate powerfully to cone C. Perform five times, increasing the intensity with each repetition so that the final two are performed at full speed.

REACTIVE STARTS

Run at moderate speed toward cone B, then, on a signal, accelerate as fast as possible to cone C. Perform four times. The signal can be varied and made soccer specific (for example, reacting to a ball).

PARTNER-REACTIVE STARTS

Two players stand side by side with one in a lead role and the other in a following role. Both players start to move at the same time, but the following player is not allowed to get ahead of the lead player. At any point before cone B, the lead player accelerates to cone C. The following player reacts to this sprint and tries to reach cone C ahead of the lead player. Perform six times.

Jockeying

ATHLETIC POSITION

Assume an athletic position while receiving and passing a ball. Perform four sets of 20 seconds each.

KNEE TAG

Two players face each other and attempt to tap each other's legs between the knee and hip. Players must use rapid foot and hip adjustments in order to make and avoid the tags. Repeat eight times for five seconds per round.

PROTECTING THE SPACE

Two players face each other with a cone positioned five yards (or meters) behind them. One player attempts to reach the cone while the other uses his or her body and appropriate movements to stop the first player. Perform eight sets of five seconds each.

GETTING FREE TO RECEIVE

Two players face each other in a box that is 10 yards (or meters) square. One player is the attacker, and the other is the defender. The attacker tries to create space to receive a pass from a player outside the box. The defender tries to either stop the attacker from getting free or intercept or prevent the pass. Perform 10 attempts, 5 as attacker and 5 as defender.

Acceleration

SINGLE-EXCHANGE WALL LEG LIFT

Lean against a wall while assuming a straight-line posture. Raise the left leg forward and up. Drive this lead leg into the ground, simultaneously driving the opposite leg forward and up. Pause for two seconds then repeat with the other leg. Repeat this sequence for a total of five drives by each leg.

ARM ACTION

Stand in a square position. Drive one arm powerfully backward so that it reaches a point level with the hip. Drive the opposite arm forward so that the hand comes to shoulder level. Alternate arms back and forth for four seconds. Rest for 10 seconds and then repeat this sequence five times.

STANDING-START DRIVES

Assume an effective starting position. Using a driving acceleration action, sprint forward for 10 yards (or meters). Repeat six times (twice to the front, twice to the right, and twice to the left).

REACTIVE SPRINTS

Assume an effective jockeying position 10 yards (or meters) outside the penalty box and be ready to react in any direction. When a ball is played, sprint forward and shoot the ball into the goal. Repeat five times.

Changing Direction

180-DEGREE RUN-IN AND CUT

With two cones placed five yards (or meters) apart, run from cone A to cone B. At cone B, plant the outside foot in a cutting action and sprint back to cone A. Perform five times for each leg.

RUN AND CUT

With two cones placed five yards (or meters) apart, run from cone A to cone B. On approaching cone B, decelerate and then perform a powerful lateral cut with the right foot and accelerate away to the left. Repeat using the left-foot cut to accelerate away to the right. Perform five times in each direction.

RUN, FEINT, AND CUT

Begin with the same procedure indicated for the run-and-cut drill. This time, however, just prior to the cut, shift the body weight briefly in the direction opposite of the intended movement. Then cut powerfully and accelerate in the intended direction. Perform five times in each direction.

GETTING PAST

With two cones placed five yards (or meters) apart, one athlete takes an offensive role at cone A while the other takes a defensive role at cone B. Athlete A attempts to get past athlete B by using the moves practiced in the run, feint, and cut drill. Further specificity can be added by having another player feed the ball in to athlete A, who tries to score while athlete B tries to defend against the feed. Players should switch roles after each attempt and perform the exercise six times in each role.

Gamespeed is a skill and therefore can be enhanced through deliberate practice. One key to developing this skill is to target either a specific movement capacity (such as acceleration) or a specific task (such as getting free). Using the target movement syllabus allows us to identify key movement capacities, and the target mechanics allow players to apply optimal technique.

In addition, the RAMP protocol allows us to use basic movements to raise pulse and body temperature, and the RAMP potentiation phase allows us to increase the intensity of movement application. Adding degrees of freedom then allows us to progress the cognitive challenge until the movements resemble those deployed in soccer.

Part II
Technical Speed

Passing

In today's game, as it is played at the highest levels, teams can combine for as many as a thousand passes per match. In addition, some teams (for example, Barcelona and Bayern Munich) regularly make more than seven hundred passes of their own. These possession figures are remarkable, but there is even more to the story. In these games, players regularly achieve pass success rates above 90 percent; some even attain 98 percent success (and occasionally 100 percent) over a 90-minute encounter. Indeed, in qualifying for the World Cup in 2010, Spain achieved a pass success rate of 88 percent for the team!

Other club and international teams have reached similar levels of success as retention of possession has become a key feature of modern soccer. Will this focus continue, or will early penetration gain emphasis and become the first thought in a coach's mind?

In today's English Premier League, for example, the number of passes made has almost doubled since 2002. Clearly, a shift has taken place, and the game is played today with great focus on continuous passing and controlled possession.

Of course, many passes in today's game might not be viewed as being made at speed. However, as play nears the opposition penalty area, or as quick attacks and counterattacks develop, many passes are in fact made at speed—and with little time for addressing the ball or preparing the feet and lower limbs to release the ball effectively. Indeed, the modern game requires that players be able to deliver passes within two seconds of receiving while using an average of two touches.

Thus the challenge for coaches is to give the players of tomorrow all that is needed to play in this speedy manner. In short, the question is this: How do coaches help players attain 90 percent pass success rates while playing at speed with minimal time for decision making? It is no easy matter to design practice sessions that meet both the needs of the talented player and the requirements of the game at the highest levels. In order to succeed, we must create practice sessions that are deliberately focused on meeting these demands. After all, the game in the years to come is unlikely to slow down or be less technically demanding!

PASSING TECHNIQUE

Passing the ball is the focal point of attacking soccer, yet there are few "pass masters"—those players who can supply teammates with the precise pass they require, over any distance, in any circumstance, and at the right moment. Many good orthodox passers can be found, but those who can deliver passes with spin, varied trajectory, and appropriate pace are worth their weight in gold.

Players in possession of the ball in today's game face a variety of challenges. High speed and sustained pressure from opponents test the player's ability to move the ball quickly in rapid but accurate pass sequences that deny and defeat the pressure. When teams vacate their own attacking half in order to defend deep, the challenge may be different. In this case, passing speed may be relatively slow when approaching the opponent's defending half, but in order to penetrate a defending block of players, attackers must use speed, change of speed, disguise, and a variety of passes.

Instant Passing

Today's speedy game requires players—especially those in the middle and attacking thirds of the field—to release the ball to others *now*. If the playing situation demands that the ball be delivered instantly, then the player needs to have developed the necessary instant-passing skills. Thus it is crucial in practice sessions for players to pass the ball in restricted space in high-intensity settings. To make this possible, coaches must design and operate practice and play situations that require the player to quickly recognize passing outlets and execute passes immediately. Indeed, passes delivered with little backlift and address to the ball are regular necessities in the modern game—and will be even more so going forward.

Players must often minimize the time between their first receiving touch and the following contact to release the ball. Again, at the game's highest levels, the average time in possession of the ball is around two seconds, and some teams try to reduce that interval to less than one second when doing so is advantageous. The demand to pass the ball so quickly requires players to develop their ability to pass in unorthodox and even unusual ways—perhaps when off balance or with little or no time to organize the feet and body in order to make the required clean contact. As a result, "any surface, anytime, anyhow" must be the slogan for the player developing the art of accurately passing the ball in all circumstances.

Any pass, of course, must be delivered for the benefit of the receiver. With this in mind, players become invaluable if they develop not only the skill to pass instantly but also the necessary speed, spin, drag, and flight to be accurate. To appreciate what mastery of flight, spin, and delivery can do, we need only watch the likes of the two Argentinean players Juan Riquelme and Juan Sebastian Veron—as well as others, including Paul Scholes, Andrea Pirlo, Xabi Alonso, and David Silva—who can deliver the ball instantly, accurately, and with all the necessary qualities.

The passing repertoire displayed by these players is exceptional in the types of pass, the distances, and the necessary "applications" to the delivery in the form of factors such as pace, flight, and spin. So the ability to deliver *now*—over any distance, without hesitation, and with the necessary range and feel—is a skill set that any would-be high-level player must acquire.

These realities of today's game make clear that restricting younger players to developing orthodox, ordinary, and obvious passing skills (even if used with confidence and consistency) also limits their future effectiveness at the highest levels. Many a player with these credentials has operated successfully but lacked the intricacy, unpredictability, and sheer cleverness to be truly inspirational and to generate in others that feeling of total admiration and wonder.

Therefore, when young players are challenged to develop the true art of passing, they must be encouraged, protected, and supported as they reach for these advanced skill levels. At the same time, they must be immersed in controlled, customized, and focused practices, as well as free play that provides the opportunity for both success and failure. Only through consistent and regular exposure to these types of practices—combined with a player's own yearning to reach the highest passing level—will he or she be able to achieve consistent passing excellence.

One- and Two-Touch Passing

The modern game is characterized (and the future game will be also) by regular, rapid sequences of accurate, high-speed passing in which three or four players touch the ball minimally, usually only once. Players use these passing sequences in response to such situations as being pressed vigorously by opponents, needing to bypass opponents at speed in midfield areas, negotiating a crowded penalty box, and, of course, playing counterattack soccer.

The ability to use rapid pass sequences to penetrate quickly and accurately will surely remain a necessity as teams defend deeper and concentrate eight or nine players and the goalkeeper in their own half. This rapid-pass tactic is used regularly, for example, by both Barcelona and Arsenal as part of their attacking strategy. In another example, when Manchester United won the Champions League in 2008, 68 percent of its goals scored in free play (that is, not in set plays) resulted from players using only one or two touches en route to the goal scorer. This is just one example; the same approach is a common feature of modern soccer played at the highest levels.

Fortunately, players can develop this aspect of their game through practice activities focused on passing, receiving, and ball retention skills—for example, the 3v1 possession game (see page 95). This drill covers most of the necessities for helping players appreciate the factors involved in keeping possession of the ball over a short range. It provides an excellent introduction for younger and youth-age players and is also effective with highly-skilled young players. In this practice, players try to receive and pass the ball with a maximum of two touches whenever possible. In order to succeed, players need to quickly support the player in possession and get into position where the ball can be passed to the feet or to a space near a moving player's feet (see figure 5.1).

Figure 5.1 Support players in a position where the ball can easily be passed to their feet or near their feet.

Because players in this practice are under pressure from defenders, they must be able to use any part of either foot to perform a "tight" first touch and to release the ball. These techniques should be encouraged and taught, since it is often crucial to minimize the time between the first and second touches. Doing so requires an efficient and appropriate first touch to set up the ball for the pass.

This practice can be extended in a variation called 3v1 high-intensity possession (page 96), which develops quick and accurate passing under pressure. In this version, in order to maintain constant pressure on the attacking players, three defenders work together to apply pressure.

Another extension that can be used is double 3v1 possession (page 97), in which two games of 3v1 are played in an area that is 10 x 10 yards but can be adjusted to 15 yards (or meters) square according to player capabilities. In this version, eight players occupy the area, and each of the two attacking teams works to retain possession of its own ball with the aim of using no more than two touches wherever possible. Retaining possession for a specific number of passes in this drill is a challenging goal, especially since each attacking team not only operates in the restricted area but also faces added interference from the other attacking group.

If players intelligently use one touch to pass accurately, they should be recognized and praised by the coach. Of course, when the player in possession faces severe pressure from an opponent, he or she may need to use more than two touches to protect the ball and possibly dribble past the defender (see figure 5.2). Whatever the necessity, then, the player should recognize what must be done—release the ball to someone else, retain the ball personally, or destroy the pressure with a dribbling skill—and

Figure 5.2 Player protecting the ball when under severe pressure by an opponent.

play intelligently. Thus, with help and guidance from the coach, this drill enables players to develop intelligent decision-making ability.

To increase the level of challenge yet again, the north–south–east–west activity (page 98) adds the dimension of direction into the practice. In this practice, one team of four players tries to move the ball against two opponents along a north–south axis while another team of four tries to move its ball on an east–west axis in the same area. Each team tries to play the ball to target players positioned behind its respective end line.

This drill puts a premium on passing the ball simply with minimal touches and appropriate speed according to the situation. It also severely tests the quality of a player's first controlling contact with the ball. To challenge players even further, use five attackers for each team working against three defenders in a slightly enlarged playing area.

This type of practice is highly relevant to today's game. In the crowded central areas of the attacking third of the field (or any congested area), players need the ability to make rapid decisions and deliver the ball quickly while moving at high speed in various directions. To do so, they must prepare and shape the body and feet appropriately for delivering passes instantly and accurately. They must also be able to touch, deflect, or pass the ball with any part of either foot and then perhaps create space to receive the return pass.

These skills need to be ingrained in players' minds, especially for those who operate in and from midfield areas and are often required to take over the role of forward players. These players must also master the added ingredient of deception. Even though many of today's passes are quicker to reach their target, today's defenders also read situations and use improved speed to react rapidly against the intended receiver. Even so, they can be deceived by players who perform the unexpected.

This context allows us to see that the north–south–east–west practice nearly replicates an actual game situation. Teammates are available to receive passes, defenders operate together in a confined area, and other interferences arise (in this case, from the other game taking place at the same time) as players move into position as needed. As a result, the activity tests players in multiple areas of their game: their ability to make correct decisions (and change their decisions as needed); their mastery of the art of delivering obvious, orthodox passes at different speeds in a small area; and their ability to deliver unorthodox, unpredictable passes.

Despite the need for speed, the ability to pass the ball with two quick touches (rather than a single touch) is beneficial in various situations. For example, if the receiver is not immediately open, the ball holder needs an extra split second before releasing the pass. In other cases, the defender arrives quickly at an angle that takes away the route of the would-be one-touch pass. As a result, in confined and crowded areas, players need to have mastered the art of passing with the second touch, after using the first touch to set up a passing opportunity or to protect the ball from an opponent.

When faced with quick-pressing defenders, a player who can use the first touch to keep the ball close to his or her feet (within immediate playing distance) not only protects the ball if needed but also sets the ball up to release a pass instantly when required. This ability allows teams to play quick two-touch soccer as well as the rapid one-touch sequences mentioned earlier. The technical secret here lies in that close and accurate first touch, followed by the instant release of a pass with any foot surface as required (see figure 5.3). Top-class teams can use these skills to move the ball at such a pace and with such consistency and fluency that defenses become dislocated and defenders find it almost impossible to succeed.

To help players develop these skills, the 50-up practice (page 99) gives two teams of equal number the chance to operate with quick passing in a

Figure 5.3 In two-touch soccer, a player must *(a)* keep the ball close to the feet with a tight first touch and *(b)* instantly release the ball for a pass.

congested area where a tight first touch is a likely solution to evade pressing opponents. When attacking, each team is aided by two neutral players who join whichever team has possession at any given time. This practice activity challenges each team to accumulate 50 successful passes before the opposing team does.

Now, it is highly unlikely that any team, operating against a similarly talented team in a congested area (even with two extra players when attacking), can total 50 successful continuous passes before the opponent takes possession. So the aim of the game is to stack up as many consecutive passes as possible in a given possession on the way to a total of 50 over the course of multiple possessions. For example, a team might score 10 passes, followed by perhaps 12 passes completed by the opposing team, followed by another 10 passes completed by the first team, and so on. The first team to total 50 successful passes wins the practice.

Deceptive Passing

Passers who can hide or disguise their intention before contacting the ball often help the intended receiver by earning him or her a split second or an increase of space in which to receive the pass. To do so, passers can look elsewhere and shape their body and feet convincingly to suggest a different intent from their real one, thereby confusing defenders and increasing their chance of threading a pass through a narrow space (see figure 5.4).

Intelligent players understand that any deception must be convincing but not overly exaggerated. The passer must leave the opponent feeling certain of his or her intent before doing something different, which may require no more than a late and slight deviation of the angle of the passing foot onto the ball just before the contact. The essence of deceit is the apparent naturalness and normality of the expected behavior when in fact the passer is actually doing something different. Whether the technique involves a feint before a pass, a cross, a dribble, or a shot, the deceit must be convincing and subtle to succeed.

Thus deception is a key skill, but do coaches teach it? Surprisingly, in all my experience, only a couple of coaches have deemed this cleverness worthy of inclusion in the teaching process. However, though standard and predictable technique may be the staple ingredient of the game, deception is invaluable in those inevitable moments when the game demands clever invention.

This reality raises a key question: Can disguise be added onto a simple, acquired passing technique at a later stage of development, or should it be included as an integral part of a player's efforts to develop technical range? If a player is to develop the skill of deception completely and naturally, I believe that it must be taught from an early stage, so that it becomes an

Figure 5.4 *(a)* Disguising the passing intent and *(b)* deceiving the defender, forcing him off balance.

ingrained part of the player's skilled performance that he or she can call upon without hesitation when needed.

Indeed, deception is such a valuable and necessary element in the modern player's repertoire that unexpected and unusual passing skills are rapidly becoming features of the game at high levels. For example, the reverse pass (see figure 5.5), the back-heel pass (see figure 5.6), and other uncommon passes are sure to become more of a necessity as players in possession seek to deceive the defense. Any coach who does not appreciate and address this reality does a disservice to players who hope to participate at the highest levels.

Figure 5.5 Reverse pass.

Figure 5.6 Back-heel pass.

Happily, the art of deception can be taught, encouraged, and developed through the use of any themed passing or possession practice. For example, the five practices discussed thus far in this chapter can involve the coach in teaching and praising players' success in using accurate deceptive passes where appropriate.

Another useful activity for teaching deception is the unusual passing drill (page 100) which offers a simple introductory practice for developing clever passes. In this practice, players take control of the ball, run at a controlled speed, and, at the appropriate time, deliver a pass to the next player using a reverse pass. For example, the ball might be passed with, say, the right foot moving across the body and the ball being passed to the side and behind the body of the passer.

Another pass that can be used in this practice is the step-over back-heel. Here, the player runs with the ball, steps over the ball at his or her feet, and makes contact with it using the back of the heel, thus directing the ball backward at an angle to reach the receiver (see figure 5.7). In fact, with imagination and understanding, a coach can devise various unusual and clever practices that involve both ground and aerial passes to open players' minds to the many possible methods for releasing passes.

Figure 5.7 Step-over back-heel pass.

To increase the challenge, the clever passing drill (page 101) encourages players to use a variety of clever passes under varying degrees of pressure. In this drill, two teams of equal number play against each other inside a circle with alternating help from two neutral players who join whichever team is in possession at the moment. The diameter of the circle should be 50 yards (or meters) if the teams number seven members each; adjust the diameter as appropriate for different numbers of players. Each of the four goals are some 10 yards (or meters) away from the circle perimeter, and an arc of mannequins defends the goal.

In the practice, teams try to score by passing the ball over the mannequins and into the net, either directly or on a single bounce. Attacking players are put under pressure by opponents and therefore must operate quickly as they receive the ball and set up the first touch to aid the delivery of the ball if necessary. The key here is the player's ability to measure or "range" the pass and the amount of force and backspin (if any) needed to lift the ball over the mannequin barrier and into the goal.

Passes can be delivered into the goal from as far away as 50 yards (or meters) and from as near as 10 yards—if the ball is "chipped" to ensure that it climbs quickly over the barrier and then enters the goal. After each attempt, regardless of whether it succeeds or fails, the coach serves another ball into the practice immediately in order to keep the action moving. However, the coach should not be reluctant to halt the practice at times if he or she sees that players could use specific information or education to aid their understanding and performance.

This practice also offers another benefit for today's and the future type of soccer. As teams defend in deeper positions, attacking players need the ability to penetrate a block of defenders with both ground and aerial passes. With that in mind, this practice gives players a chance to practice and refine the intelligent and creative passes they need to make in order to succeed under such circumstances.

A typical deep-defending organization is illustrated. To breach the back defending line, the attacker may well have to deliver a clever and unexpected pass. Attacker 4, in possession of the ball, is confronted by a pressing defender and may now thread the ball between defenders 3 and 6 to release the ball to wide attacker 7. If attacker 4 broadcasts the intended pass to attacker 7 by his or her body shape (indicating that the pass is about to be delivered), defender 3 may well read the situation, anticipate the pass, and intercept the ball.

However, if attacker 4 suggests a pass to attacker 10 but then passes to attacker 7 with the outside of the right foot while looking at attacker 10, defender 3 may be surprised. Alternatively, if attacker 4 looks toward attacker 7 before final contact on the ball, he or she might well deceive defender 5 and then deliver an unexpected aerial pass to attacker 10.

Coaches sometimes encourage clever, creative dribbling skills but spend less time on promoting the value of deceptive and unusual, but accurate, passing skills. Yet the ability to pass with this kind of deception and "feel" when contacting the ball is an asset for any player, and younger players should develop it as part of their early work on passing skill. The practices that have been devised and illustrated give players and coaches the opportunity to move toward high-level passing skills. With this approach, while working on the orthodox facets of passing the ball accurately, coaches and players should not be afraid to experiment with passing skills that are unusual and creative.

Figure 5.8   Deep-defending units.

Passing in Tight and Congested Areas

As the game has evolved into its modern form, more teams have chosen to defend with eleven players positioned between the halfway line and their own goal, as shown in figure 5.8.

Figure 5.9 shows a not-uncommon defensive phase of today's game. Teams frequently defend deep, with as many as nine players and the goalkeeper defending their goal in the final third (of the pitch. Penetrating this defensive organization can be difficult even for the best teams, but both individual players and teams will have to find answers to this now-familiar challenge. No matter where the ball is transferred, defenders group together and deny their opponent the opportunity to penetrate the defensive block. As a result, successful attacking play

Figure 5.9 Striker's options for passing the ball when defenders play deep within the final third of the field.

requires that a team be capable of operating successfully in congested areas of the pitch (see figure 5.9).

The art of deception can come into play in various parts of the field. Not only are passing requirements becoming more challenging during central approach play in the middle third and in the areas just outside the penalty area but in addition, as the game evolves, more teams now prefer to pass the ball into the penalty box, as opposed to delivering a long hopeful pass or cross. They also continue to pass within the penalty box with awareness, perception, and craft in order to produce scoring opportunities. In such situations, shooting feints may be employed to attract and commit a defender to a challenge before making a simple pass to a teammate who holds a more favorable scoring position (see figure 5.10).

Modern attacking play also requires players in or around the penalty box to provide ever-moving targets for passes. No longer can strikers simply take up a position and hope that a cross will be delivered from the flanks or that a pass will arrive. To the contrary, especially during central attacking play, modern attackers constantly reposition themselves and take into account the positions and likely actions of defenders in order to provide passing outlets for the player in possession. Thus mobility, agility, and quickness are prime requirements for attacking players who function in and around the penalty box.

This necessity, however, tells only half the story. Upon receiving the ball, a great striker must also make the correct decision about whether to strike at goal, hold the ball, turn, or provide another player with a scoring opportunity. And the possibility of providing others with scoring opportunities

Figure 5.10 Shooting feints force a defender to commit, creating passing outlets.

takes us back to our initial proposition that passing to others is both a changing and a challenging art. In order to "lay the ball off" to a teammate, those who are selected to become strikers must possess the necessary cleverness and subtlety for passing in confined and crowded playing areas. Indeed, redirecting the ball to another player when tightly marked with little available space will be an increasingly important attacking skill. As with other players, strikers need to develop their ability to release the ball with complete control over its speed, accuracy, and trajectory while moving at various speeds.

Figure 5.9 indicates an example of the possible options for a striker during an attack to "lay the ball off" with precision and intelligence. The striker must be skilled at recognizing a variety of angles, employing different contact skills and controlling the speed, timing, and accuracy of the maneuver. He or she must also have the ability to "take the sting out" (reduce the speed) of incoming passes before providing accurate passes for others.

As defenses congregate and compact in the defending third of the field, the space between defenders is reduced, and the distance between the goalkeeper and rear defenders is also shortened. Therefore, in order to supply attacking players who operate within or adjacent to the central goal-scoring areas, passers may need to deliver the ball with more pace than usual in order to penetrate the corridors between defenders. Indeed, even those narrow corridors will be filled quickly by the best defenses, which react and reorganize rapidly against opponents who move the ball quickly.

To breach the gaps, passes must often be played with disguise and with little backlift or address in order to be "punched" rapidly through an available space and reach their target within or behind the defense. Strikers, then, need to develop the skill of relaying passes that arrive with extra speed (fast incoming passes) to other supporting players, often using only one touch and various surfaces of the foot so that they may strike at goal (see figure 5.11).

Figure 5.11 When challenged by defenders, strikers must be able to use different foot surfaces to release incoming passes in congested areas.

In addition, though it may be preferable to receive these fast passes to the feet, some passes require the receiver to redirect the ball to a teammate by means of another body surface (see figure 5.12). Therefore, strikers must be particularly quick at arranging their feet and body in order to guide the ball to others. Likely examples include bending at the knees to pass the ball with the chest, raising one foot to drop-volley a pass, and bending at the knees to deflect the ball with the head.

This ability to both deliver and receive fast passes in tight areas will surely become an increasingly common feature of attacking play. Another vital skill will be that of redirecting and deflecting incoming fast passes with deftness and in any direction with one touch.

Players can practice these skills through the lay-offs drill (page 102). This simple activity develops players' ability to quickly find others who are supporting them through a variety of angles and services, such as quick

Figure 5.12 Strikers especially must use the *(a)* head, *(b)* chest, or *(c)* thigh to redirect the ball.

passes to the feet and chipped passes to the chest. Though we have discussed such skills in relation to attacking play in and around the penalty box, the need to deliver and redirect passes also applies in midfield areas and to defenders penetrating the midfield ranks of opponents to supply forward players with fast ground passes.

We have also discussed the quality of deception in the delivery of passes, and never will this quality be more useful than in tight and congested areas of the pitch. In fact, the quality of deception is a great asset not only in delivering passes but also, as discussed in chapter 6, in receiving the ball.

In midfield areas where opposition teams withdraw and defend deep, players must be able to pass the ball quickly when opponents pressure the ball holder and potential receivers. Attacking midfield players also need that tight first touch, quick pass release, and ability to pass with one touch over various distances. In addition, high-class players in midfield possess the ability to hold the ball at the feet and release it once the opponent has fully committed to a challenge. In fact, clever midfield players can deliberately wait for an opponent to challenge for the ball before releasing it to another player or moving with the ball away from or past the challenging defender. When waiting for the opponent to strike for the ball, they often give the impression of biding their time while scanning for a pass receiver with their head up in a relaxed mode.

Clever players see everything but reveal nothing. They pretend to be attracted to one option but actually focus on another that is more beneficial without letting others know it. They keep a secret! Then, just as the opponent is attracted toward the ball, they release a quick unexpected pass to a teammate, often followed by a quick movement to receive the ball once more via a wall pass. If this pass is played past the opponent toward the goal at a striker's feet, the return pass puts the midfield player in position to attack the last defending line, either with a pass or by running with the

ball. If the midfield player in possession of the ball faces the side of the pitch, the defender is often more committed to pressing—feeling that the ball holder will not pass behind him or her but rather will pass the ball square across the field—and so moves closer.

If the ball holder positions the ball on the outside of the foot nearest the defender, this maneuver exposes the ball and may well encourage the opponent to challenge for the ball (see figure 5.13). If, instead, the ball is held on either the inside or the outside of the foot farthest from the opponent, doing so may encourage him or her to move even closer in an effort to press and force an error (see figure 5.14). As the opponent moves

Figure 5.13 A player can entice a defender to challenge a ball exposed on the outside of the foot closest to him.

Figure 5.14 Keeping the ball on the (a) inside or (b) outside of the foot farthest from the defender forces the defender to move in closer. But the ball is still protected with the body.

close and commits to the challenge, the ball is released past or in some cases over the tackling foot. Great players may also entice the defender to strike at the ball by dragging it in toward their body with the sole of the foot as they slowly move backward.

As the defender closes in and challenges for the ball, the player in possession toe-lifts the ball over the challenging foot to a teammate (see figure 5.15) and moves quickly past the defender—often to receive a return pass, or simply to support the next receiver. In fact, when pressed vigorously, high-class midfield players are equally adept at releasing the pass beyond the opponent with any part of either foot. They also possess the ability to deceive an opponent with body positioning, false scanning with the eyes, and head turning, and they understand how such deceptions are likely to cause defenders to react.

Figure 5.15 Player *(a)* positioning the ball to *(b)* toe-lift it over the defender's foot.

Inventive Passing

Great players possess dependable fundamental skills, and the basic and orthodox passing skills come easily to them. But in those moments when the game situation calls for something different—something creative or imaginative—clever players come to the fore. The hallmark of these outstanding technicians, with their inventive minds, is their ability to conjure up a response to the situation that few others would expect. But even though many coaches devote time and thought to developing simple, efficient passing practices, few venture beyond to encourage and develop the imaginative techniques and skills that can make the difference in a big moment.

As a result, when confronted, for example, by a thicket of defenders around the edge of the penalty box, many players look for the simple and possibly square pass to a teammate in the hope that he or she has an alternative route to an attacker's feet in the penalty box; alternatively, they may simply choose to strike hopefully at goal. However, even in this situation, some exploitable space may remain between the defending back line and the goalkeeper, and a steeply chipped pass might provide an unusual—but feasible—option for penetrating to the back of the defense.

With the ball being close to the feet, as it often is with great players in tight and pressured situations, the player needs only minimal time to bring the foot to the ball and chip, wherein the toes are quickly snapped under the ball with a short backlift of the lower leg (see figure 5.16). As shown in figure 5.17, the player could also toe-lift the ball over defenders by sliding his or her toe end under the ball before lifting it steeply over any crowd of players (using technique demonstrated in figure 5.16). As explained earlier, players can experiment with these types of passing in the clever passing practice.

Figure 5.16 The player chips the ball over an opponent by quickly snapping the toes under the ball.

Figure 5.17 Being clever around the box.

As the game continues to develop, and defenses pack into the defending third of the field (especially the central areas in front of the penalty box), players will need inventive alternatives in order to create scoring opportunities. In fact, this kind of creative passing skill is already common among South and Central American players. For example, when I was coaching the England under-17 team in a tournament in Brazil, a young Mexican midfielder passed the ball in a way that I have not seen any young player achieve either before or since.

Indeed, whether performing a high-speed run, facing a crowd of defenders in the penalty area, responding to a pressing defender, or enjoying a large degree of freedom, this player always had the solution. His technical dexterity was unsurpassed, and his quick thinking and ingenuity were incredible. He could chip, float, bend, and drive passes at will, and he possessed an ingrained ability to deliver 50- and 60-yard (-meter) passes with the outside of either foot with little address.

Of course, he must have developed this range of expertise in a variety of ways—mainly, I suppose, through engaging in regular free play, perhaps with friends, as well as working under the tutelage of a coach who encouraged invention, and spending considerable time in deliberate practice from a young age. The results were obvious in his admirable courage to try unorthodox (for most players) passing solutions, confidence in his own ability to do so, and intelligence in deciding on the solution.

The challenge for coaches lies in understanding that this type of imaginative passing is not merely a luxury but, increasingly, a key to success in penetrating defenses and creating scoring opportunities. As a result, coaches must provoke players' imagination and encourage and develop their confidence in using these creative arts. Indeed, such passes as the back-heel, the step-over back-heel, the steeply-chipped pass and other less common passes should be part of the technical development curriculum for younger players.

Another innovative way to pass is through volley passing, which players can practice by using the drill of the same name (page 107). When it is impossible to find routes through or around the defense, players may yet find alternative routes *over* the opponent, which can require players to pass the ball while it is in the air (see figure 5.18). Few coaches have their players practice this skill formally; they simply expect players to acquire it through trial and error. Yet it will be increasingly important as opponents continue to press the ball quickly and vigorously and as compacted defenses challenge players to find instant but accurate alternatives to ground passing.

The orthodox volley passes (with both the inside and the top of the foot) will still be used, but players will also need the ability to pass the ball aerially with any surface of the foot and with the front and outside of the thigh. Not only that, but headed passes (see figure 5.19) and chest passes (see figure 5.20) are also on the menu for the creative passer.

Figure 5.18 Volley pass.

To make successful volley passes, players need to possess fine judgment in ranging the pass, awareness of both the receiver's and his opponent's position and movements, and the ability to apply either backspin or top spin to the ball as appropriate to the situation.

To be sure, the player who makes clever and risky, yet inventive passes may hear dismissive comments from many coaches, such as "circus soccer" or "fancy tricks," but he or she will be a great asset to any attacking team. Whether the pass is a simple and orthodox volley or one played with the outside or heel of the shoe or volleyed overhead in an overhead scissor kick

Figure 5.19 Headed pass.

Figure 5.20 Chest pass.

(see figure 5.21), an intelligent and practiced player can use the right move at the right time and thus increase his or her value to the team. The real challenge for coaches, then, is to devise realistic and inventive practices that allow and even encourage players to develop creative aspects of their game.

With this in mind, the volleys at goal drill (page 108), which is somewhat similar to volleyball, helps players develop the skill of volleying at goal using various methods. The drill is particularly valuable for strikers and midfield players who enter into scoring positions, but of course many teams move tall defenders into the penalty box at set plays, so they could also be involved in volleying at goal. More generally, all players on a team should understand the appropriate use of the volley pass—especially defenders, who, when they are under pressure, often clear an intercepted pass or cross with height and distance rather than by using an accurate volley pass with the feet, chest, or head to ensure possession.

Though passing the ball with the chest is not unusual, it is often refused as a one-touch passing alternative; instead, the player often controls the ball with the chest before taking a following action. As a result, even if the next touch results in a volley pass, the immediate advantage may be lost,

Figure 5.21 Overhead scissor kick.

and the player may therefore be forced to perform an even more complex skill in order to solve the problem.

Demand for the clever and less common passing skills discussed here will only increase as individual defenders continue to get quicker and defenses get harder to expose. Players will look increasingly to inventive passing skills to create scoring opportunities, whether in midfield approach play, quick attacking play, or play in the heavily defended penalty areas. Indeed, already, we need only to study the play of today's outstanding attacking teams to see that, when rapid counterattacking is impossible, they still have the ability to creatively build an attack and penetrate a packed defense often involving clever, unusual and unorthodox skills to do so.

The long pass will also continue to feature in effective attacking play, though perhaps not in the way that some would expect. Many a team's game plan has been built on the cornerstone of frequent long passes (over 50 to 60 yards or meters). Unfortunately for many teams, however, delivering these long passes regularly, even when under immense pressure and in difficult circumstances, has often resulted in a loss of possession as opposing defenders make first contact on the ball.

Teams have tried to solve this issue by immediately regaining possession from the defenders who were under pressure on contacting the ball, which to some observers is an unwelcome and unpopular way of playing the game. In some cases, the use of numerous long passes has driven opponents deep into their own defending third and thus shifted the location in which possession is contested to that area of the pitch. In this use of the long pass, accuracy is not paramount, though it remains desirable. It is hard to imagine this style of play continuing to be employed at the highest levels of the game. However, the tactical and timely use of the long pass most certainly will persist.

Indeed, whether the long pass is used to launch or continue a counterattack or to serve as the final pass, it will always be useful in attacking play. The art of the long pass lies not only in ranging the delivery but also in the quality of delivery. Thus players must explore and practice a variety of long passes—for example, the long straight-driven pass that slows as it arrives at the receiver, the pass delivered with backspin, and the pass delivered with both backspin and sidespin into restricted space.

Indeed, it is a skill of the highest order to deliver the long pass instantly over 60 yards (or meters) with minimal address and backlift of the kicking foot. If a player can deliver this pass with either foot, and with both the inside and outside surfaces of the foot, then attacking players ahead of the ball can make well-considered and incisive movements knowing that the supply is likely to arrive.

Similarly, players who can deliver the long pass from different angles into the goal-scoring areas—avoiding the goalkeeper and defenders with well-calculated flight and pace—will be invaluable in unlocking well-organized and compact defenses. For example, zonal defenses that require the fullback to support the center backs by moving into semi-central positions will struggle to defend the long diagonal pass from left to right (or vice versa) from, say, a central back to a flank player on the other side of the field, especially when it is delivered early and with pace. Therefore, players, especially defenders and midfielders, must prioritize developing their ability to make this long pass with all the appropriate qualities, including the art of deception.

To develop these abilities, players can use the long-range passing drill (page 109). Of course, the dimensions of the practice area can be adjusted according to the age and developmental stage of the players involved. For instance, for a simpler version, a coach could pit three players against one defender at each end of the practice setup and reduce the passing distance to suit the players' age and capability.

Passing on the Run

As counterattack becomes an even more prevalent tactic in modern soccer, players increasingly need the ability to run at speed and release passes over a variety of distances from that run. As opponents defend deeper and in numbers, one solution is the rapid attack that seeks to produce a scoring opportunity before the defense recovers into its chosen structure. Upon gaining possession of the ball, the two most threatening options for the attacker are that of releasing and that of running with the ball.

When a player chooses to run with the ball, the time it takes to cover ground while moving toward the opponent's defensive area can be a deciding factor in the success of the counterattack. In order to increase their efficiency in traveling with the ball, players must attend to the quality of the touches they apply. If those touches are uncontrolled (either too short or too long), the player loses fluency in moving with the ball.

At some stage in the break forward into space, the player in possession must make a decision either to continue running with the ball or to release it to someone else. Therefore, players must master the difficult skill of passing the ball accurately while running at optimum speed. While running with the ball on counterattack, the player must observe the actions both of other attackers and of defenders, since these factors dictate where, when, and to whom the player should release the ball.

When approaching defenders or restricted space, the player may well reduce pace and therefore stride length in order to ready the body and feet to release the pass or dribble past an opponent. It is difficult to feed the ball to teammates with the necessary quality when moving at speed, and arranging the body and feet to release the pass gives defenders vital clues about the likely recipient and timing of the release. This is no problem, however, if the attacking player has freed himself from a defender's attention and simply needs the pass to be played simply and accurately. To develop the skill of running with the ball and releasing passes, players can use the running with the ball drill (page 111).

There are also times when the ball holder should put defenders at a disadvantage by disguising his or her intended pass with a look at an alternative possibility. As we have seen, looking in one direction and releasing the ball in another is a classic means of putting defenders at a disadvantage even when moving at speed in a counterattack.

In addition, passing the ball with the outside of the front foot provides less early information to defenders than passing with the inside of the foot (see figure 5.22). The natural flow of the running cadence is less interrupted if the player makes contact with the ball on the outside of the foot in the last stages of the stride and just before the foot is planted on the ground. In contrast, releasing the ball with the inside of the foot often requires the attacker to turn the hips and lower leg in order to contact the ball, which interrupts the running cadence and makes it less fluent. In addition, clever defenders read this body language and are thus alerted a split second earlier to the intended pass receiver.

Thus counterattack success requires players to release passes with the outside of the foot over a variety of distances while running at speed. These passes are often dispatched to attackers who are also moving into space at speed, which makes it crucial for passers to exercise good judgment in choosing the pace of the pass. The pass must often travel between defenders and thus needs extra pace to bypass them before an interception can be made. The passer's challenge, then,

Figure 5.22 Passing the ball with the outside of the foot helps to disguise the pass.

is to apply the required skill, speed, and spin to the pass so that it eludes the immediate defenders but does not carry to other defenders or to the goalkeeper, who may be acting as a sweeper behind the defenders.

More specifically, the passer must address multiple important considerations—the angle at which to deliver the pass (to avoid the goalkeeper's and other defenders' sweeping range), the speed of the pass, and the drag or backspin applied to the pass. Drag or backspin may be needed to cause the ball to slow down in the latter stages of its travel in order to avoid would-be interceptors. Applying all of these factors—moving at optimum speed, using appropriate deception, releasing the ball off the front foot, and applying the necessary spin and pace—makes the difference between success and failure.

Alternatively, passes may be made to stationary or almost stationary targets with a view to receiving a return pass, as in a wall pass. The pass is made to the feet of the receiver after taking into account the position of any marking defender, and in this case the need for spin and other qualities is not as crucial. Other needs—for accuracy, disguise, and fluency of the run both before and after the pass—remain the same, and the preparatory stage before the release is unlikely to differ much from that of passing into space while moving at speed. Players and coaches can use the running-with-the-ball combination play drill (page 112) to practice running with the ball and possibly combining with fellow attackers before releasing the final pass.

In summary, because the game is becoming quicker, attacks are also quick and initiated instantly. As a result, succeeding at the highest levels of the game requires players to perform skillfully, accurately, and appropriately at speed. Therefore, releasing the ball while running at speed is a vital skill that needs regular practice.

Passing Under Physical Pressure

When defensive areas of the pitch become congested, players in possession of the ball who are put under severe pressure by opponents may not be able to release the passes they wish to make. When this happens, of course, they need to find alternatives. At the same time, defenders may continue to pressure the ball, closely accompanying the ball holder wherever he or she chooses to take the ball in the quest to find a suitable pass outlet. This type of pressure often requires the attacker to move across the pitch with the ball in search of pass options while facing determined opponents who press aggressively but fairly.

Nonetheless, attackers who possess good ball manipulation skills may well escape a defender's unwanted attention by using a clever and unexpected skill to "shake off" the opponent. Doing so usually involves making a sudden change of pace and direction in order to create space in which to lose the defender; in addition, the change may be aided by setting up some sort of disguise movement.

If this attempt to get free fails, or if the ball holder lacks the technical range to even try it, then he or she must look to release the ball, knowing that some degree of body contact may be made with the defender in the process. In this case, the ball holder can protect the ball to some extent by keeping it on the outside of the foot farthest from the defender as it is moved across the pitch. In the meantime, the defender is likely to challenge for the ball or make body contact with the player in possession. In preparation for this pressure, the attacking player can brace his or her body while leaning into the opponent's challenge as the pass is delivered. This situation will become more and more common as opponents drop deeper defensively and compact the areas in and around their own defending third of the field.

Players in these situations are required not only to withstand the buffeting from their opponent but also to deliver passes with deft touch and accuracy while having little time or opportunity to address the ball and prepare their feet and body to release it. These skills—passing and even receiving the ball despite physical contact—are rarely taught to our younger players, but they can be developed through any kind of man-to-man practice game. For example, in the passing under pressure drill (page 114), attacking players become accustomed to the physical presence of, and even contact with, opponents.

When attacking in this practice, players should know the position and movement of their immediate marker as they prepare to receive and then actually receive passes. They may have to protect the incoming pass by placing their body between the ball and the defender. If their timing and execution are good, they may turn away from the defender's contact as the defender attempts to challenge for the ball and makes some degree of physical contact with the attacking player. Alternatively, an attacker in possession of the ball with his or her back to the defender might use a clever feint or movement over or around the ball to put the opponent off balance and enable an escape—albeit taking some physical contact from the adversary.

Thus this practice often challenges attackers to operate when defenders are close to both the attacker and the ball. Such conditions challenge the player's ability in multiple areas—to use a close-controlling (tight) first touch, to turn, to feint as if performing one skill while actually performing another, to eliminate an opponent alone by dribbling, and to bypass defenders using combination play with teammates.

This type of practice can also nurture a player's ability to lose defenders in order to receive the ball to the feet or into space. In addition, players must be able to wait for the right moment to change direction and speed before moving to receive a pass or combine with the player in possession. These demands mean that players who are static, unimaginative, slow moving, or slow thinking are unlikely to succeed in this practice. They should be encouraged to operate with more intensity and speed at the appropriate time and will need educating on how to do so. It offers the opportunity, however, for attacking players to acquire a high number of attacking skills while being opposed constantly.

This practice also helps defenders develop multiple key skills—marking an opponent, reading and intercepting passes, pressing and challenging for the ball at the right time, tracking opponents, and, indeed, nearly all individual defending skills. In fact, in my work as a coach with most age groups, including senior professional players, I have always found this practice to be more than useful for developing the individual and combined skills and tactics outlined here.

PASSING DRILLS

This section describes all of the practices mentioned in the preceding discussion. These descriptions provide coaches with the seeds to develop appropriate practices for their players and, where necessary, to raise the challenges to even higher levels.

3v1 Possession Game

Purpose

Developing quick, accurate passing skills

Organization

Set up an area that is 8 to 10 yards (or meters) square. Identify three attackers and one defender. One attacker starts with the ball.

Procedure

1. One attacker starts the practice with the first pass, which is allowed by the defender, and then the game begins.

2. Using a maximum of two ball touches, attackers try to retain possession against the defender for 20 consecutive passes.

3. If the defender intercepts a pass, he or she switches roles with the attacking player who made the pass unless the coach chooses to have the defender operate for a specific amount of time before a change.

4. No passes may be made above knee height.

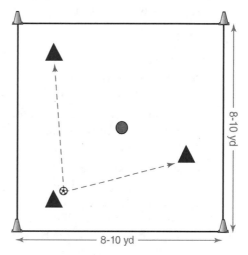

Coaching Points

- Support the ball holder where his or her pass can reach the receiver's feet.
- Upon receiving the ball, be aware of movements by the defender and support players.
- Within two touches, release a pass to a teammate and provide support.
- If appropriate, use one-touch passing to find a support player.
- If using two touches, remember that first-touch quality is vital and should be used to make the pass easier and quicker to release if necessary.

3v1 High-Intensity Possession

Purpose

Developing quick, accurate passing skills

Organization

Set up an area that is 8 to 10 yards (or meters) square. Identify three attackers and three defenders, two of whom are waiting outside the practice area. One attacker starts with the ball.

Procedure

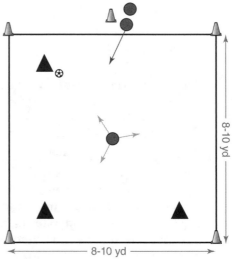

1. Play is started by one attacker passing to another before the defender becomes active.

2. One defender presses the ball for a short period (about 10 seconds) of high-intensity defense.

3. After 10 seconds, as the play continues, the original defender is replaced by the second defender, who applies high-intensity pressing until being replaced by the third defender with this sequence continuing.

4. Attackers attempt to retain possession under the high-intensity defense for 30 seconds or more as indicated by the coach.

Coaching Points

- Support the ball holder where his or her pass can reach the receiver's feet.
- Upon receiving the ball, be aware of movements by the defender and support players.
- Within two touches (or, if possible, one), release a pass to a teammate and provide support.
- If using two touches, remember that first-touch quality is vital and should be used to make the pass easier and quicker to release if necessary.
- Make quick decisions under pressure.
- Assume quick and accurate support positions for one-touch play to succeed.
- Release the pass accurately under pressure as needed with any surface of the foot.
- First touch may be the pass or the controlling touch before the release of the next pass.

Double 3v1 Possession

Purpose

Developing quick, accurate passing skills

Organization

Set up an area that is 8 to 10 yards (or meters) square. Form three teams—two teams of three attackers and one team of two defenders. One player on each attacking team starts with a ball.

Procedure

1. Play is started by the attacker in possession of the ball passing to another member of his team before the defenders become active.

2. One defender presses the ball to gain possession against each attacking team.

3. Each attacking team tries to retain possession for 12 consecutive passes.

4. After 12 successful passes, one player from each attacking team switches roles with the defender.

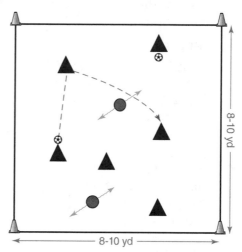

Coaching Points

- Focus on your own 3v1 game despite interference from players moving in the other game.
- Create or find the largest possible support space.
- At all times, be aware of all players' movements as you prepare to receive or release a pass.
- Once the pass has been released, create a further support position.
- Try to disguise your passes to deceive the defender—for example, look at one target but deliver to another.
- Use a variety of passes to find a support player.
- Vary the speed—but never the accuracy—of your passes

Variation

To increase the difficulty, extend the playing area and use 12 total players (rather than eight) to play two games of 4v2 rather than 3v1. Also include two resting defenders who can replace the pressing defenders as necessary.

North-South-East-West

Purpose

Developing quick, accurate passing skills

Organization

Set up an area that is 20 yards (or meters) square. Form two attacking teams of four players each and two defending teams of two players each. One attacking team against two defenders play north–south, and the other attacking team plays east–west against their defenders. In addition, position one target player behind each end line as illustrated. One player on each attacking team starts with a ball.

Procedure

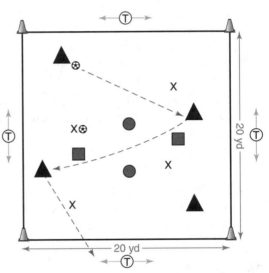

1. Play is started by one of the attackers passing to a team-mate before the defenders become active.
2. Each attacking team tries to play the ball in the appropriate direction to the target player behind its end line.
3. When a team succeeds, the target player returns the pass, and the attacking team then plays in the opposite direction.
4. Each attacking team tries to move the ball from one target player to the other as many times as possible in two minutes.

Coaching Points

- When moving to receive a pass, be aware of opponents, spaces, and support players.
- Upon receiving a pass, turn whenever possible to increase the possibility of passing forward, either through or past the opposition.
- Pass quickly, accurately, with deception if necessary, and with sensitivity to the needs of the receiving player.
- Eliminate defenders with individual dribbling ability or combined play (such as wall passes).
- Whenever possible and appropriate, run with the ball at spaces or opponents to move play forward.

Variation

To raise the difficulty level, enlarge the playing area and increase the number of players to enable 5v3 play on each axis (north–south and east–west). Also include resting defenders who can replace active defenders after 20 seconds to maintain practice intensity.

50-Up

Purpose

Practicing one- and two-touch passing skills

Organization

Set up an area that is 30 yards (or meters) square. Form two teams of seven players each and identify two neutral players. These elements can be flexed as needed. The challenge for the coach is to arrange a playing area that is appropriate for the players' age and ability yet creates congestion for the number of players involved. One player on the attacking team starts with the ball.

Procedure

1. Play starts on the coach's command.

2. Teams accumulate a total of 50 successful passes before the opponents do so.

3. The two neutral players assist whichever team is in possession of the ball.

4. If the ball leaves the playing area during play, the coach serves a new ball, either to the team that had possession (if the opponent caused the ball to leave the area) or to the opponent (if a misplaced pass or faulty ball control caused the interruption).

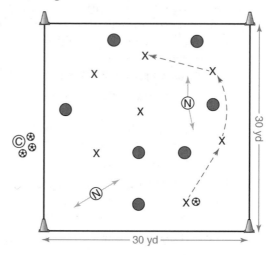

Coaching Points

- Find as much space as possible in which to receive passes.
- Upon receiving the ball, be aware of the positions and movements of both teammates and opponents.
- Decide early (but remain open to changing the decision quickly, if necessary) who should receive the pass.
- Pass accurately with as few touches of the ball as possible.
- If needed, deceive opponents before passing the ball by shaping the pass to one player but delivering it to another.
- Use a variety of foot surfaces to release passes when necessary.
- Execute combination plays (such as wall passes).
- Run at spaces with the ball before releasing or feint to pass but continue running.

Unusual Passing

Purpose

Making clever and unusual passes

Organization

Set up an area that is 25 yards (or meters) square. Position nine players as shown in the diagram. Player 1 starts with the ball.

Procedure

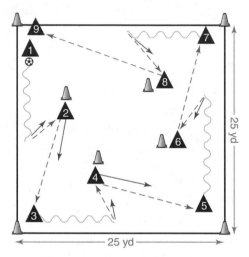

1. Player 1 starts play on the coach's command by running with the ball at a controlled speed before passing to player 2 using either a reverse or a back-heel pass. Player 1 then takes player 2's position.

2. Player 2 receives the pass from player 1 and executes a one- or two-touch pass to player 3. Player 2 takes player 3's position.

3. Player 3 runs with the ball before delivering an unusual pass (reverse or back-heel) to player 4. Player 3 takes player 4's position.

4. Player 4 executes a one- or two-touch pass to player 5. Player 4 takes player 5's position.

5. The sequence continues for the rest of the players. The practice continues for a period of time before a rest.

6. Upon completing the sequence, players work back in the opposite direction.

Coaching Points

- Run with the ball at speed but under control.
- Arrange your feet and body appropriately to deliver a reverse or back-heel pass to the next receiver.
- Deliver other unusual or unorthodox passes with accuracy and deception.

Clever Passing

Purpose

Making clever and unusual passes

Organization

Set up a circular playing area that is 50 yards (or meters) in diameter. Place each of four goals 10 yards from the edge of the circle as illustrated in the diagram. Place a semi-circle of mannequins in front of each goal. Form two teams of seven players each and identify two neutral players who play for the team in possession.

Procedure

1. The coach initiates play by feeding a ball in to one of the teams.
2. The team in possession tries to score by delivering the ball over the mannequins and into any of the four goals from a variety of distances.
3. The team in possession retains the ball until a player can receive the ball and deliver it into the goal.
4. After a goal the coach feeds a ball to the team that made the goal. If a failed attempt (the ball misses the goal), the coach feeds the ball to the other team.

Coaching Points

- Upon receiving the ball, calculate the distance to the goal and choose a correct method of delivery into the goal (chip over shorter distances, drive over longer distances, lift over very short distances, or bend around opponents).
- For high-level passing excellence, the pass should bounce before entering the goal after traveling over the mannequins.

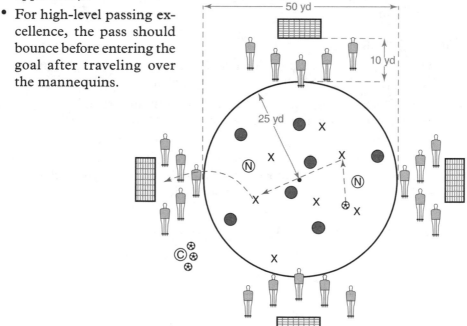

Lay-Offs

Purpose

Passing with minimum touches

Organization

Set up a circle that is 40 to 50 yards (or meters) in diameter. Around the outside of the circle, position five players. Inside the circle, position two teams of two players each. One player on the outside of the circle starts with the ball.

Procedure

1. The player with the ball passes it to player 9 inside the circle.

2. Upon receiving the ball, player 9 uses one touch and passes to player 10 inside the circle.

3. To receive the pass from player 9, player 10 moves at speed and in various directions.

4. Player 10 passes the ball to an outside player, who then returns it inside the circle to the first player on the second team. (The first pair inside the circle rests while the second group works.)

5. Play continues as outlined in the preceding steps.

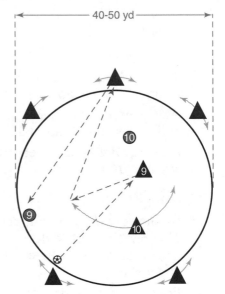

Coaching Points

- Outside players should use various passes at various heights and speeds when delivering the ball to the inside players.

- Player 1 should move at different speeds and in different directions before receiving the pass and should anticipate both the pass delivery and the support player's run.

- The support player 10 should move in different directions in order to support player 9 and even move out of his sight occasionally to challenge his or her ability to find the support player with minimal touches.

- Players inside the circle should work at speed to develop their ability to pass with various body and foot surfaces.

Mixed Passing

Purpose

Developing passing skills

Organization

Set up one area that is 18 yards square (or meters) square; around the outside of that area, set up a larger area that is 25 yards square. Position four attackers and two defenders in the inside area. Position five additional attackers, one at each corner of the outside area, with two starting at one corner with the ball. One target player is along each end line of the outside area as illustrated. In both the inside area and the outside area, one attacking player starts the practice with a ball.

Procedure

1. Play starts on the coach's command, and the two players with a ball each pass to a teammate.

2. In the inside area, players perform a 4v2 skill practice in which the attackers try to keep the ball away from the defenders for one minute.

3. In the outside area, players practice their passing technique as follows:

   1. Attacker 1 passes the ball to target player 1, then runs forward to receive a pass before passing to attacker 2 and following the pass to become attacker 2.

   2. Attacker 2 receives the ball, passes to target player 2, receives the return pass, and then passes to attacker 3 and follows that pass. Players continue this pass-receive-pass-follow sequence around the square for a specific amount of time.

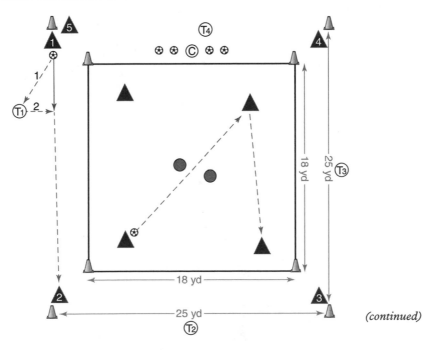

(continued)

Mixed Passing *(continued)*

Coaching Points

Inside area:

- Assume early, quick support positions to be accessible for passes.
- When passing the ball, use only one or two touches if possible.
- Disguise passes and use both feet and various body surfaces to release and receive passes.

Outside area:

- Pass over distances of 5 to 10 yards (or meters) when passing to target players and 20 yards when passing to the next receiver.
- Turn after receiving a pass at one of the corners of the square playing area.
- Pass with both feet and various foot surfaces and occasionally use disguise.

Directional Passing

Purpose

Passing in congested areas

Organization

Set up an area that is 30 yards (or meters) square with a 10-yard end zone at each end. Inside the area, position two teams of seven players each, as well as one neutral player. In each end zone, position a target player.

Procedure

1. The coach initiates play by feeding a pass to a member of one team.

2. The teams play against each other and involve the neutral player as needed.

3. The team with the ball tries to move it to a target player.

4. Upon receiving the ball, the target player has two touches to return a pass to the team that passed the ball to him or her.

5. The team then attacks in the opposite direction in an effort to move the ball from end to end for six consecutive attacks.

6. If the opposing team gains possession, it can play to either target player and then, if successful, attack the other end with its next possession.

Coaching Points

- Be aware of and work to create space for receiving passes.
- Understand the circumstances in which the ball is received (for example, man-marked, loosely marked, free).
- Pass to the advantage of the next receiver.
- If possible, when receiving the ball, turn toward the direction in which the team is attacking.
- Pass or run with the ball to make forward progress.
- Use both feet and various body surfaces to receive and release passes.
- If under pressure with no immediate support, retain and protect the ball.

Man-Marked Passing

Purpose
Passing when closely marked in congested areas

Organization
Set up an area that measures 30 yards long (or meters) by 25 yards wide with an additional 10-yard end zone at each end as illustrated. Form two teams of seven players each. In addition, position one target player in each end zone.

Procedure

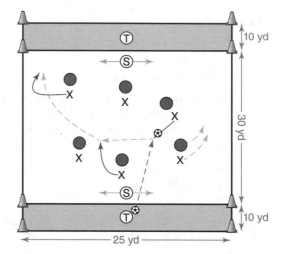

1. Play begins when the coach feeds a ball to one of the teams.

2. The teams play against each other, defending with man-to-man marking and a sweeper (free player). The sweeper can change places with a teammate after each three-minute period.

3. The team with the ball tries to move it to the target player in the end zone. If successful, the team then defends against the opposing team, which tries to pass the ball to the target player at the other end.

4. Upon receiving the ball, the target player passes to the sweeper (free player), who uses a maximum of three touches to pass to a teammate and can then support the attacking play as it develops. As the practice develops, the target player can be allowed to feed the ball not only to the sweeper but to any of his or her attacking players.

Coaching Points
- Create space for receiving the ball from the free player (the sweeper) or target player under less pressure and at the correct time.
- When receiving the ball, know your circumstances—the positioning of your immediate opponent, other defenders, and your teammates.
- Pass effectively to other tightly marked players.
- Use combination play with teammates, such as wall passes and pass-and-support sequences.
- In a 1v1 situation, attack your immediate opponent and eliminate him or her through the use of appropriate techniques, such as clever footwork, dribbling skills, and feints.

Volley Passing

Purpose

Practicing volley passing

Organization

Set up an area that is 10 yards (or meters) square. Identify three attackers and one defender. One attacker starts with the ball.

Procedure

1. Play begins when the player with the ball passes it to one of the other attackers.

2. The attackers try to keep the ball away from the defender by means of ground passes. The defender can challenge for the ball during this phase.

3. After the fifth successful ground pass, a player lifts the ball off the ground with his feet and makes an aerial pass (volley) to the next receiver.

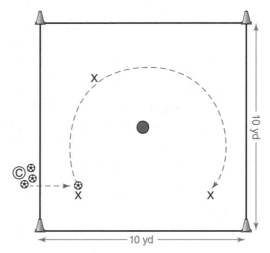

4. The attackers then try to make five consecutive volley passes. The defender can intercept volleyed passes but cannot challenge for the ball during this phase.

5. After five volleys, the ball is returned to the ground, and players try to make another five consecutive ground passes while keeping the ball away from the defender, who can now challenge or intercept passes as before. Should the passes be intercepted, they are returned to the attackers who commence the practice once again. Should the ball go to the ground before the five consecutive volley passes are made, the ground passing sequence begins once more followed by the aerial passes.

6. Players continue the sequence; there is no time limit on this practice.

Coaching Points

- When making volley passes, use one or two touches to move the ball.
- Use both feet and various body surfaces to receive and make volley passes.
- When receiving or releasing a pass, be aware of the defender's movements.
- Move the feet quickly to get into a comfortable position to either set up an aerial pass for oneself or volley to another player with one touch.
- Depending on the defender's position and movement, use volley passes over or to the side of the defender.

Volleys at Goal

Purpose

Practicing volley passing and scoring

Organization

Set up an area that measures 20 yards (or meters) by 10 yards and establish one 10-yard zone at each end. Position a portable goal at the middle of each end line and two other goals on the sidelines, at the bottom left and top right, as shown in the diagram. Position a goalkeeper in each goal and a row of mannequins across the center of the area. Form two teams of three players each. One attacking player has a ball.

Procedure

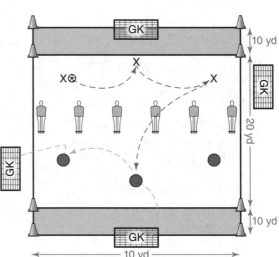

1. The player with the ball serves to a teammate, who controls the ball and volley-passes to a teammate. Volley passes can be made from the feet, thighs, chest, or head.

2. Players volley-pass to each other (with a maximum of three touches by any player) before passing the ball over the mannequins to the other team.

3. When the ball arrives over the mannequins, the receiving team can do any of the following:

   1. Overhead scissor-kick to score in an end-line goal.
   2. Volley or side-scissor-kick to score in a sideline goal.
   3. Volley-pass to another teammate to keep the ball in the air before passing it back across the mannequins.
   4. If the ball falls to the ground, a point is scored by the opposing team. The first team to score a predetermined number of points wins.

Coaching Points

- As the practice develops, challenge the team receiving the ball over the mannequins to use one touch to score using a volley, an overhead scissor kick, or a side scissor kick.
- Reading the flight of the incoming pass and adjusting the body and feet before striking the ball are crucial to success.
- The courage and ambition to leave the ground with both feet in order to perform an aerial strike at goal are necessary to score an exceptional goal.

Long-Range Passing

Purpose

Practicing long-range passing

Organization

Set up an area that measures 60 yards (or meters) by 20 yards and divide the length into three 20-yard sections. Position four attackers in each end zone, two defenders in one end zone, and two defenders in the middle zone. One attacker has a ball in the end zone with defenders.

Procedure

1. Play starts when the coach passes a ball to one of the four attackers opposed by the two defenders in the end zone or one attacker with the ball is allowed to pass to another before the defenders become active.

2. The attackers play against the defenders in the end zone and create opportunities for a long pass over the middle zone to the most distant receiver, who must be on the end line of the zone.

3. As the long pass is delivered, the two defenders in the middle zone now defend against the four attackers in the far end zone, while the original two defenders recover to and rest in the middle zone.

4. The attackers try to make six successful long-range passes from one end zone to the other

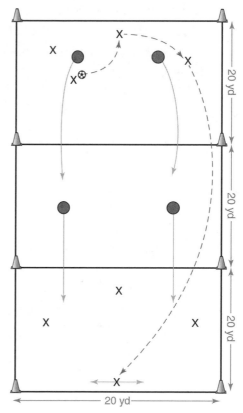

without losing possession. Should the defenders intercept the long pass, they return it to the team that attempted the long pass and continue the practice. If the long pass is inaccurate or too long and leaves the practice area, the coach restarts the practice by feeding another ball to the group of four who made the long pass.

(continued)

Long-Range Passing *(continued)*

Coaching Points

- Spread out within the zones to create space and time in which to receive the ball.
- Always know and understand the defenders' positions, movements, and intentions.
- Use the first controlling touch to set up the ball in a position from which to deliver the long pass with the chosen foot.
- Range the pass, the needed force and trajectory, to eliminate all defenders and deliver the ball accurately to the receiver on the end line.
- If necessary, use spin on the ball.
- Develop the ability to use either foot and both the inside and outside foot surfaces.

Running With the Ball and Passing

Purpose
Running with the ball and passing

Organization
Set up an area that measures 35 yards (or meters) by 10 yards and divide the length into three sections: two 10-yard end zones and one 15-yard middle zone. Position three attackers and one defender in the starting end zone and two attackers and one defender in the other end zone. One attacker in the starting end zone has a ball.

Procedure

1. The attacker in possession of the ball passes to one of the two other attacking players opposed by a defender.

2. The attacking team tries to retain possession against the defender within the 10-by-10 area.

3. Any of the three attackers can run with the ball out of the end zone and across the middle zone.

4. Upon entering the other end zone—and thus becoming the third attacker in that zone—the aim of the player in possession must be to play the ball to a receiver on the end line either directly or through one of the other attackers in that zone.

5. Play then continues in the opposite direction.

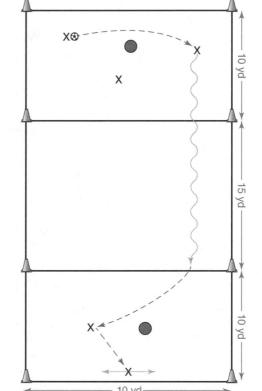

Coaching Points

- Be aware of key factors involved in retaining possession in 3v1 play: support position, passing accuracy, and quality of the first touch.

- If possible, upon receiving a pass, direct the ball with the first touch into a favorable position to run with it beyond the defender.

- After the first touch, use stronger touches for more distance and accelerate more quickly and fluently with the ball across the middle zone, keeping the head up.

- Where possible, run with the ball, contacting it with the outside of the foot.

Running-With-the-Ball Combination Play

Purpose

Running with the ball and passing

Organization

Set up an area that measures 35 yards (or meters) by 10 yards and divide the length into three sections: two 10-yard end zones and one 15-yard middle zone. Position three attackers and one defender in the starting zone and two attackers and one defender in the other end zone. Position one attacker and one defender in the middle zone. One attacker in the starting zone has a ball.

Procedure

1. The player in possession of the ball passes to a teammate in the same zone.

2. The attacking team tries to retain possession against the defender.

3. Any attacker with the ball can run and initiate either of the following in the middle zone: (1) join the attacker in the middle zone, where combination plays are encouraged, or (2) enter the middle zone and pass to the middle zone attacker, who then moves with the ball into the other end zone and passes to the player on the end line.

4. Play continues in the opposite direction.

Coaching Points

- Be aware of key factors involved in retaining possession in 3v1 play: support position, passing accuracy, and quality of the first touch.

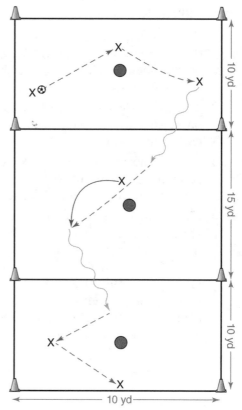

- If possible, upon receiving a pass, direct the ball with the first touch into a favorable position to run with it beyond the defender.

- After the first touch, use stronger touches for more distance and accelerate more quickly and fluently with the ball across the middle zone, keeping the head up.

- Upon entering the middle zone while opposed by the defender, use various techniques, such as wall passes, overlaps, and feints and swerves, at speed to retain possession while running into the end zone.
- Where possible, when running with the ball, use the outside of the foot to make contact with the ball.

Variation

This practice can be further developed by positioning four attackers against two defenders in the starting end zone, two attackers and two defenders in the middle zone, and three attackers and two defenders in the other end zone. The purpose remains the same—running with the ball and using passes and combination plays to defeat defenders.

Passing Under Pressure

Purpose

Passing and receiving the ball despite physical contact

Organization

Set up an area that is 25 yards (or meters) square. Form two teams of equal number (4v4, 5v5, or 6v6). In addition, position one target player on each sideline and one on each end line (for a total of four target players).

Procedure

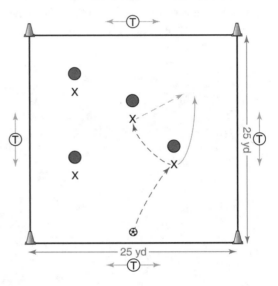

1. Practice begins with one of the target players passing the ball in to a player on one of the two teams.

2. The teams oppose each other on a man-to-man basis. Each tries to move the ball from end to end five times in a row.

3. Target players on the end lines play with the team in possession and are free to move anywhere along or behind their line in order to provide support.

4. Target players on the sidelines also help whichever team has possession and can provide support from anywhere along their line.

Coaching Points

- Shake off your opponent using changes of speed and direction in order to receive the ball with more space and time.

- When receiving the ball or in possession, protect the ball by screening it from the defender.

- If possible, turn to face the defender and try to eliminate him or her by using dribbling skills or working in combination with other attackers (for instance, using a wall pass).

- When not in possession of the ball, provide support for the pass.

Penetrative Passing

Purpose

Developing quick and accurate penetrative passing skills

Organization

Set up an area that is 30 yards (or meters) square. Form two teams of six players. The goalkeeper plays within a 10 yards in diameter circle, and no other player is allowed inside the circle. There is also one neutral player.

Procedure

1. The teams of six and one neutral player, who plays for the team in possession, play to and pass to the goalkeeper from outside the circle whenever possible. The team without possession cannot enter the circle occupied by the goalkeeper.

2. After receiving the ball, the goalkeeper throws it out to a member of the team who passed the ball to him.

3. The first team to pass to the goalkeeper on 10 possessions wins the challenge.

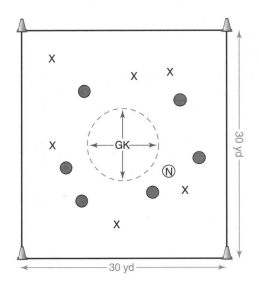

Coaching Points

- Spread out as a team when in possession of the ball.
- Pass quickly and accurately when pressed by the defending team.
- See and take opportunities to pass to the goalkeeper either with passes played between the defenders or over and around them.
- It may be necessary to pass the ball quickly for a number of passes to find a pass that penetrates into the circle.
- If the goalkeeper catches the ball, spread out as a team in order to receive his pass and have more time and space in which to play.

Receiving

As the game quickens in general, and ball speed between players increases in particular, the demands of receiving passes becomes more challenging. When fast passes are delivered, receiving players must still be able to use the first controlling touch to place the ball into an advantageous position, especially when moving at optimum speed and in different directions! Knowing exactly where defenders are, as well as their likely intent, enables the receiving player to determine the appropriate controlling touch and, if needed, to change the touch required at the last second if circumstances change.

Such passes may arrive not only at the receiving player's feet or in spaces around him or her but also at inconvenient heights. Therefore, players must be able to appreciate the amount of space available and determine the distance and direction of the first touch that is needed in order to retain control of the ball while moving at high speeds.

This awareness, or knowing quality, is a crucial element in all aspects of play—none more so than when a player is about to receive the ball. As the game quickens, the player's ability to purposefully use his or her senses during game play increasingly affects performance quality. Indeed, when great players move to receive the ball, they engage in a complex process that includes observing the flight of the ball, predicting the likely circumstances upon the ball's arrival, preparing oneself to receive the ball, calculating possible action alternatives, and choosing the prime option—and doing all of this before the first contact!

The artfulness lies in knowing everything possible but not letting others know that you know. Such knowledge enables the receiving player to, if necessary, deceive opponents into thinking that a certain action will be taken but then perform a different action.

RECEIVING TECHNIQUES

The ability to receive the ball and place it in the proper position to perform the next action has always been one of the pivotal individual skills for a player to develop, no matter the level at which he or she aspires to perform. In fact, controlling the ball is the bedrock of excellent performance whenever a player is in possession. Players at the highest levels master the incoming pass in a variety of ways, and this chapter addresses some of the perhaps unusual methods of exercising clever receiving skills. Granted, the well-founded and orthodox receiving skills must also be rehearsed regularly, but in our opinion the skills referred to here are essential for players who have the desire and capability to play at the highest levels in the future.

Tight and Soft First Touch

Once the receiver has assessed all relevant factors as the ball travels, his or her first touch on the ball is now the prime consideration. Just as there are many possible purposes for controlling the ball, the receiving player must master a range of first touches to meet that variety of needs. More specifically, as the game is increasingly played in congested areas while a team builds its attack and moves forward—and as defenders become quicker to apply pressure—attackers need a tight and soft first touch that subdues and directs the ball into a position close to the feet and possibly away from an opponent's challenge (see figure 6.1).

With this reality of the game in mind, we need to reexamine the old adage "get the ball out of your feet" when controlling it. If the intent is to run strongly with the ball into space, then this advice may well apply. In congested situations, however, time and space are at a premium, and a tight first touch is needed. By "tight," I mean that no matter how the ball arrives, the player must be able to place it within 1 yard (meter) of his or her feet—no more, and often less. If players need to play instantly, and for sure they sometimes will, the ball must be within immediate contact distance for the player to deliver the

Figure 6.1 Tight and soft first touch.

pass or otherwise take the next action which may be to manipulate the ball into a position of safety.

For example, Lionel Messi, Diego Maradona, Ronaldinho, and all the great South American players seem, as if by habit, to place the ball close to their feet (within that crucial one yard or meter), no matter how it arrives, and, if necessary, to ensure the security of the ball before taking their next action. There is no loose or heavy touch with the first contact—unless it is part of an act of deception! It is far better to possess this close touch than to never master the art of securing the ball because of a lack of understanding and practice. Better still, this tight touch provides the foundation for passing and striking skills that require little or no backlift—a sure necessity in the future game.

The tight touch, which may well be pressured by opponents, gives the attacker the opportunity to add a quick second touch if needed to evade any opponent's challenge for the ball. It also often attracts defenders close to the ball, where they may be eliminated by a quick shift of the ball away from or to the side of the challenging foot, since the ball is within easy reach after that first contact. Indeed, this first and tight touch close to the feet stills the ball, frequently stills the player in possession, and often fixes and stills the defender, as he or she respects the quality of the possession and exercises caution about the position of the ball. Rarely will a sensible defender strike at the ball when facing an opponent, unless he or she is absolutely sure that contact will dispossess the attacking player.

One example was Diego Maradona, who was a master at subduing the ball with a tight soft touch and inviting opponents to consider challenging for the ball from a close distance. Once the opponent was close and prepared to strike for the ball, he would repeatedly threaten to contact the ball by picking up his lower leg as if to strike it. He would then outwait his opponent, who would often challenge for the ball and be eliminated by a change of direction, pace, and movement with the ball. In fact, Maradona kept the ball so close to his feet that it took only a split second to make contact, and he was always ready for the challenge that resulted from his feints.

Thus a tight and soft first touch gives players the foundation to act quickly when required. Following this tight touch with a feint and a quick pass or dribble enables players to play accurately and effectively in congested areas and highly pressurized situations. Players who acquire these skills gain the ability to play into, inside, and out of congested areas competently and efficiently. Therefore, coaches who devise practices in which their players move at high speed to receive quick passes in restricted spaces and then perform related skills are serving their players well as the game evolves into the future.

The tight receiving drill (page 126) helps players develop this controlling skill with emphasis on reduced space, congested areas, and directional play. One first-touch technique that is now prominent is that of controlling the ball with the sole of the foot (or studs of the shoe.) Familiar among many South American players, this technique is perhaps a legacy of the game of futsal; regardless, it ensures that the ball is close to the feet after the first controlling touch. Though not frequently used by players moving at high speed, it is often used by players who are already in position to receive the ball or are in the latter stages of moving to a position in which the ball will arrive almost straight toward or around their feet.

Because the modern game involves not only more passes overall but also more ground passes in particular, this first-touch technique is being used by more players receiving the ball with their back to the opponent. From this position, the ball can be manipulated easily through a wide range of angles, serving as the catalyst for a whole menu of evasion skills whereby attackers move the ball slowly and close to their feet before exploding quickly in another direction.

Attacking First Touch

First touches can often be described as "passes to self." In its simplest form, the first controlling touch places the ball in position for performing a further skill that is sometimes not immediately apparent. The first touch can also be used to eliminate opponents as they move quickly toward the ball and press the receiver. For instance, the wide attacker who receives a pass as the opponent quickly closes the ball down may well use the first touch on the ball to direct it past the defender, on either the inside or the outside, as the defender arrives at speed (see figure 6.2). In this example, we see the following action:

- Midfield player 4 passes to wide attacker 7.
- Defender 3 presses the ball quickly from an inside angle, perhaps encouraging wide attacker 7 to control and hold the ball.
- As defender 3 moves close to the ball, wide attacker 7 uses the first contact to pass to himself some 10 yards (or meters) behind defender 3 and moves at high speed to the ball.
- In doing so, wide attacker 7 has already determined that no other defender can take possession of his or her pass into space.

If the wide player's action is hidden or disguised, then the defender may be taken by surprise, in which case his or her reaction time is reduced. Of course, the receiving player must direct this first touch accurately into space, and with the correct force, in order to avoid the ball moving toward covering defenders. Great players can direct the ball past defenders into space with backspin or sidespin, knowing that the ball will "hold up" for them or spin into the required position as they move to the ball. Spin can also deceive defenders.

The first touch can be played with either the inside or the outside of the foot, depending on multiple factors: the route of the incoming pass, the closing angle and speed of the defender, and the ability of the wide player to arrange his or her body and feet to execute the skill efficiently. Midfield players may well employ this same skill when

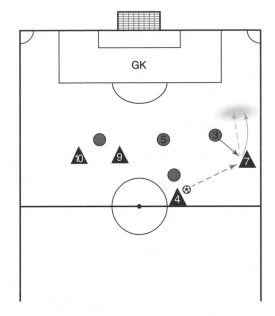

Figure 6.2 The attacking first touch.

receiving passes with their back to opponents or when receiving the ball while sideways to opponents.

This skill of bypassing an opponent with the first touch has been easily implemented by such great midfield players such as Carlos Valderrama of Colombia and Juninho Pernambucano of Brazil. The skill of touching the incoming pass at the very last moment—as the opponent commits to challenge for the ball—moving it around one side of the defender, then spinning away to the other side to regain possession, is a high-level skill that all players in attacking situations should develop with their first touch.

Inventive strikers often use the first touch with their chest, thigh, or foot to deflect the ball past, and sometimes over, a tight-marking opponent and into a striking position. High-level operators have mastered this ability to use the first touch on the ball to eliminate a tight-pressing or marking opponent and retain possession of the ball, and players who wish to play at high levels should develop this ability as well.

First-touch attack (page 127) is a simply organized drill using small numbers in which players develop their ability to use an attacking first touch to expose an opponent. This practice is particularly good for wide attackers but is also useful for other players. In addition, because this version is a no-contact practice, a young (say, 13-year-old) player can participate with players who are two or three years older and still benefit from this specialized practice.

This drill lays a foundation for the range of biomechanical movements that are required to perform the skill. Of course, decisions have to be made, but they are more technical than tactical. Introducing an opposition at a later stage furthers the practice value because it challenges the pass receiver to decide when, where, and how to use the skill and possibly incorporate feints at the right time to disguise his or her real intention—in other words, to make tactical decisions.

Deceptive First Touches

It is a valuable asset for any player to be able to use the first touch to deceive an opponent. With this end in mind, players can gain an advantage if they are aware of the situation (both near and away from the ball) as they receive the ball. For example, a receiving player might decide to pass to a support player but notice a defender screening the route of the intended pass. In response, as the ball arrives, the receiving player might direct the ball with his or her first touch in a direction and at a distance that causes the opponent to move off the line of the intended pass.

For instance, a midfield player may touch the ball to his or her right, knowing that the defender will respond by moving to the left in closing down on the ball holder (see figure 6.3). As the opponent moves to the left, the attacker in possession then passes the ball through the space vacated by the defender's response to the first touch. The farther the first touch moves from the passing route, the more likely the defender is to respond in a more expansive fashion, thus offering a wider passing angle. The art of the receiving player lies in knowing just how far to move the ball off the pass line in order to move and deceive the defender before releasing it. This kind of tactical craft and the ability to implement it are the marks of an intelligent player—and are therefore attributes that should be acquired by all players.

Successfully taking a calculated risk with the first touch makes for high-level play. Having a "bad but knowing it is a good" first touch makes for exceptional play. Having calculated the distance and movement of an opponent coming to press the ball, the receiving player can deliberately lengthen the first touch into a position that invitesthe defender to commit to a

Figure 6.3 The player touches the ball to his right, forcing the defender to commit and opening up space to pass the ball.

challenge aimed at making contact with the ball. In reality, however, the receiving player, knowing that he or she can make up the distance to the ball after the seemingly poor first touch, accelerates and arrives at the ball a split second before the defender, whose momentum is toward the ball. These deceptive skills can be developed through the first-touch deception drill (see page 128), a simple practice that allows players to experiment with feints, disguises, and first-touch differences before accurately releasing a disguised pass.

With the defender now totally committed to the challenge, the attacking player can use the second touch to eliminate the opponent and move away from the challenge or past the defender. Though I have seen this happen many times with a genuinely poor first touch, I have also seen it used intentionally by players with immaculate first-touch ability. In particular, Brazilian and Argentinean players have performed this skill too often for me to believe that it is not calculated and deliberate. With these examples in mind, coaches must encourage young players to experiment with their range and quality of the first touch—but only after they have acquired sound fundamentals, which is in itself a lengthy and challenging task for many players and coaches.

Turning Off of the First Touch

Another way to practice the craft of deception is to deceive the opponent as the ball travels and arrives. Specifically, all attacking players should develop the ability to make a late, fast turn with the ball. Indeed, though it is often good play to receive and turn early and quickly with the first touch, it can also be a clever attacking play to save the first contact with the ball until the very last second. This ploy has lured many a marking or closing defender to the ball with the expectation of making an interception or at least challenging for the ball while the attacker is seemingly unaware of the pending danger.

In reality, however, receiving players who are aware of the defender's position and movement can lure the defender to approach quickly and to a position close to the pass receiver. By allowing the ball to come to them rather than moving toward it and at the same time giving no clue that the defender's intention is known, then the defender can be put at a massive disadvantage. Meanwhile, the defender, thinking that he or she is undetected, is encouraged to strike for the ball or move close to the attacker, especially if the attacker's back is turned or if the attacker is sideways to the defender.

Such calculations involve an element of risk, but the clever attacker times his or her movements perfectly and turns on contact with the ball just before the defender arrives to challenge for the ball. The turn may be made either away from or into the defender (turning to face the defender), after which, if needed, the attacker quickly employs a second touch on the ball to evade any challenge for the ball.

The first-touch turn drill (see page 129) provides an opportunity for the receiving player who is marked closely from behind to turn late and quickly, often as the defender is challenging for the ball. It enables the receiver to keep his or her back toward the defender while turning but also allows the receiving player to move quickly away from the defender at an angle to help with the turn toward the opponent if that is the chosen skill (see figure 6.4).

Once again, this is a foundational practice that introduces and develops the technique and biomechanics likely to be involved in turning off the first touch of the ball. Receiving players in this practice can devise their own manner of turning off opponents by using feints and various foot surfaces and by touching the ball around the opponent on one side while turning the opposite way.

Figure 6.4 The receiver keeps his back toward the defender, moving away quickly and turning at an angle.

In addition, coaches can vary the location of the passing and receiving players to create a wider possible range of turns off the first touch. This enables players to practice receiving the ball not only with their back toward an opponent but also receiving passes when away from the defender and half-turned to him (see figure 6.5). For instance, changing the practice configuration to a diamond shape enables passers and receivers to practice turns off the first touch.

Of course, when half-turned while receiving the ball, receiving players could, if they calculate correctly, allow the ball to run between themselves and the defender and then move quickly to retrieve it. The later and more quickly this ploy is performed, the more it will surprise the defender. To practice alternative turns regularly in an opposed practice format, use the competitive first-touch turn drill (see page 130).

Figure 6.5 Creating a wider turn range, the player a can receive passes away from and half-turned to the defender.

RECEIVING DRILLS

The preceding discussion has explored the range of possibilities at a player's disposal when receiving the ball and some of the tactics involved in applying various receiving skills. The practices referred to throughout that discussion are presented here in some detail for coaches to explore and further develop.

Tight Receiving

Purpose

Receiving the ball

Organization

Set up an area that is 15 yards (or meters) square. Form two teams of three players each and identify one free player. One player on the attacking team has a ball.

Procedure

1. Play commences with one team having possession and making the first pass to an unopposed teammate.
2. The attacking team tries to retain possession with the aid of the free player.
3. The defending team tries to gain possession of the ball and when doing so can use the free player to assist in keeping possession.

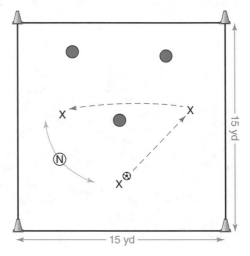

Coaching Points

- Be aware of the positioning and movements of all players.
- Put defenders off balance by feinting before making first contact and either controlling the ball or moving it in one direction before touching it in another direction.
- Prepare to receive the ball using any surface of either foot and any part of the body.
- Economize on the first controlling touch by placing it within quick playing distance—that is, use a tight first touch.
- Keep the ball close to the feet and be ready to outwit and eliminate a defender with clever passes or unexpected individual skill.
- Release passes with either foot and various foot surfaces after enticing the defender to challenge for the ball.

First-Touch Attack

Purpose

Making an attacking first touch

Organization

Set up a diamond-shaped area that measures 25 yards (or meters) by 10 yards; adjust the size as needed depending on your intention and on the age and developmental stage of the players. Position one player at each corner and a fifth player waiting to join the play. One player has a ball.

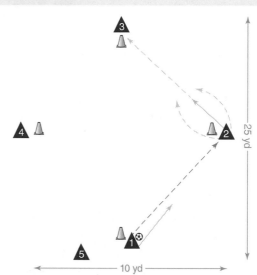

Procedure

1. The player with the ball (player 1) passes with speed to player 2 and follows the pass. The waiting player (player 5) takes player 1's place at the start.

2. Player 2, upon receiving the ball, uses the first touch to push the ball either inside or outside of the cone and then retrieves it on the other side.

3. Player 2 then passes with speed to player 3 and follows the pass.

4. Player 3 controls the ball and passes to player 4, who practices using either foot and various surfaces to deflect the ball beyond the cone before moving on to pass to player 5 who keeps the passing sequence going.

Coaching Points

- Practice both clockwise and counterclockwise.
- Use clever movement both before receiving the ball and upon receiving it.
- Experiment with using various foot surfaces to touch the ball and with varying the distance of the first touch while always being able to reach the ball before it gets to an imagined defender (or use a marker on the ground).
- Practice feints before the first contact on the ball.
- Challenge yourself to use the first touch both to lift the ball off the ground and to keep it on the ground in order to deliver different and appropriate passes.

Variation

As players progress in their mastery of this simple practice, the coach can introduce the concept of spinning the ball with the first touch. More generally, a coach who brings creativity to practice design in order to challenge players can fire their imagination and excite them to strive for high achievement in practice. In addition, of course, introducing defenders into the drill can test the attacking players' ability to both select and perform various first-touch skills.

First-Touch Deception

Purpose

Making deceptive first touches

Organization

Set up an area that is 10 to 15 yards (or meters) square. The area can be adjusted for different purposes, and a rectangle or diamond shape will also do the trick for technique and skill development. Position one player at each cone and a fifth player waiting to join the play. One player has a ball.

Procedure

1. Player 1 passes to player 2 and follows the pass. The waiting player (player 5) takes player 1's place at the start.

2. Player 2 uses a first touch to the right followed by a second-touch pass to player 3, who moves off of his or her cone to receive the pass.

3. Player 3 feeds the ball to player 4 and follows the pass.

4. Player 4 touches the ball off line and to the right before passing to player 5, who moves to receive the pass and continues the passing sequence.

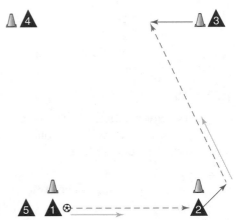

Coaching Points

- The first controlling touch can be played to either side of the body before passing to the other.

- Before receiving passes, use clever individual movements, such as feints and direction changes.

- Ensure that the first controlling touch is always made away from the intended line and direction of the next pass.

- Accompany the first touch with a feint.

- Disguise the first pass, perhaps by looking away from the next receiving player.

First-Touch Turn

Purpose

Turning off the first touch

Organization

Set up an area that measures 30 yards (or meters) by 20 yards and divide it into two 15-yard halves. Position one player at each corner cone and two players at each center cone for a total of eight players. Identify a ninth player who is waiting to join play. One player has a ball.

Procedure

1. To start the practice, player 1 passes to player 2 and follows the pass.

2. Player 2, closely marked by player 3, with his first touch of the ball turns to the side of player 3, moves the ball into position to pass to player 4, and then passes and follows the pass.

3. The marking defenders at the center cones apply varying degrees of pressure on the receiving players to challenge their response.

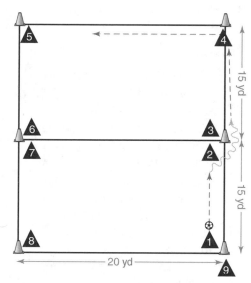

4. Player 4 passes to player 5, follows the pass and moves to the next position. When player 5 receives the ball, he continues the passing sequence.

Coaching Points

- On receiving the ball, the player turns to the right or left side of the defender with the first touch.

- Progress the practice and have the receiver touch the ball on one side, turn to the other, and collect the ball behind the marking player.

- Use both feet and various foot surfaces to turn the ball behind the close-marking player.

- Use feints just before the first touch of the ball.

- Whenever possible, turn at high speed—but under control.

Competitive First-Touch Turn

Purpose

Turning off the first touch

Organization

Set up an area that measures 30 yards (or meters) by 20 yards. Form two teams of equal number and identify one free player inside the area and a target player along each end line.

Procedure

1. The coach initiates play by feeding a ball in to a player on one of the teams.

2. The teams play against each other, and the free player joins the team in possession.

3. The attacking team tries to move the ball to a target player before receiving a return pass and attacking in the opposite direction (in order to pass to the other target player).

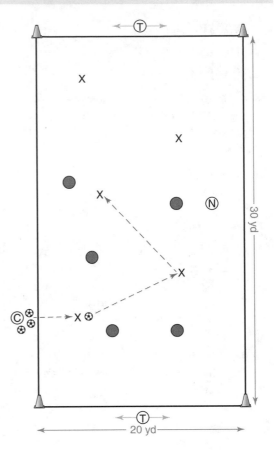

Coaching Points

- Move into a support position to receive passes.
- Know the circumstances before and as you receive the ball.
- Turn wherever possible with the ball, using the first touch to place the ball in position for passing it or carrying it forward.
- Where necessary, upon receiving the ball, deceive defenders by offering no clue that a turn will take place with the first touch.
- Save the touch and the turn until the last moment, then turn quickly in order to move the play forward.
- If tightly marked when receiving the ball, turn off or away from the defender in order to move behind him or her if possible.

chapter 7

Dribbling

To many observers, the art of dribbling is dying. Of course, there are still some outstanding dribbling players operating at the higher levels of the game. For example, Lionel Messi, Cristiano Ronaldo, and Sergio Aguero can each attack a space or an opponent with the ball at their feet and bypass any opponent in their path. In today's game, however, defenders are athletically quick, have advanced agility capabilities, are able to turn quickly and are trained in acceleration speed. Allied to these physical factors, many teams defend in numbers in their own defending third, condensing the area available in which to dribble past one opponent before a second or third defender contests and possibly steals the ball. That is not to say that dribbling is now no longer part of the game. It most certainly is and should be developed and encouraged with young players. Dramatic, clever individual skill can "open defensive doors" that combined play may not.

To a large extent, dribbling can be understood as evading or confronting a nearby opponent, or as carrying the ball at a space with the knowledge that doing so will attract an opponent. In essence, it involves changing speed or direction (or both) at the appropriate time in order to eliminate an opponent. In reality, of course, dribbling is much more complex than this simple description suggests, but for practical purposes coaches can approach the art of dribbling as revolving around those three factors—changing speed, changing direction, and doing so at the appropriate time.

Good dribblers recognize and understand the circumstances that surround them as they move into position to receive the ball. Key considerations include the movement and proximity of their immediate opponent, the presence of support or recovering defenders, the available space in which to operate, and of course the speed and height of the incoming pass. It is also crucial for a player to understand his or her personal abilities and preferences.

When one thinks of the great dribblers—in addition to Messi, Ronaldo, and Aguero—the names of Stanley Matthews, George Best, and Diego

Maradona come quickly to mind. These players have all had the courage and confidence to risk possession by attacking opponents. Their success, and that of all great dribblers, hinges on mastering the art of touch at different speeds.

DRIBBLING TECHNIQUES

Touch here refers to the precise amount of force needed to shift the ball over a shorter or longer distance in order to move it outside the range of a defender's challenge. Dribblers also use touch to slightly alter the position of the ball in order to move a defender into a position from which he or she has great difficulty regaining balance and countering the dribbler's move. In addition, when teams drop deep to defend and thus create congestion, players who want to dribble effectively must have the ability to contact the ball with different surfaces of the foot at different times as required by the circumstance.

The congested dribbling drill (page 138) helps players learn to use controlled and accurate touches on the ball while moving at varied speeds and through congestion. Indeed, in congested areas, where the defense is compact and defenders can move quickly to help each other, the ability to make quick decisions and respond to the ever-changing spaces and circumstances separates the good dribblers from the great. The great ones are constantly aware of their opponents' movements and are able to adjust their own speed, direction, touch, and balance as they negotiate their way through a compact defense.

When necessary, great dribblers also "set up" an opponent before beating him or her. Toward this end, one skill often used by dribblers is that of moving with the ball under control toward the space to either side of the defender, then escaping on the other side with a rapid change of speed and direction (see figure 7.1). Great dribblers also attack opponents directly, taking the shortest possible route toward and almost into the defender's feet, before possibly feinting and then exploding past the defender on either side with the ball.

Great dribblers maintain a watchful eye and always seem to know when the opponent is off balance and in poor position to counter a move. They also calculate the perfect time to change direction and speed. In particular, it is a joy to watch South American dribblers' ability to change their pace in moving with the ball toward a space or opponent before eliminating the opponent. Indeed, we have seen wide attackers walk with the ball at their feet toward an opponent, tempting the opponent to strike for the ball, before suddenly accelerating rapidly to one side and away. This ability to walk, wait, watch, and then shift the ball is a clever skill, but the key to success with this maneuver often lies in the ability to explode at the appropriate moment.

Of course, success also depends on the distance from the defender prior to the ball movement and explosion. The great dribblers have the courage to move to a position almost within touching distance of the defender before making the decisive move to beat the opponent. Thus success ultimately involves a variety of factors—distance from the defender, timing of the move, understanding of the proper route, and appropriate ball touch distance. Additionally, an awareness and understanding of the circumstances around the opponent and the risk involved will also come into the equation.

Figure 7.1   The dribbler sets up the defender *(a)* by moving toward the space to the right of the defender, and then *(b)* with a fast change of direction he is able to *(c)* beat the defender.

If the dribbling player can use a feint before changing direction and exploding, then the move is almost unstoppable. This method of dribbling is a common feature in South American soccer, but, despite its effectiveness, it is less seen in European soccer. Instead, because of the higher speed of games played today, many dribblers now approach spaces or opponents at speed before attempting to go past the opponent. Arjen Robben of the Netherlands is a great example of this. Therefore, the change of speed is seemingly less pronounced than in the South American game, though it is still significant. Any change of direction to go past the defender is often accompanied by a prior movement of the feet and body over or around the ball, or a quick shuttling of the ball between the feet, before making the final touch that moves the ball past or to the side of the opponent.

When clever dribblers are denied the space they need, the best create their own route past an opponent by using feints or quick ball manipulating skills. For example, a right-footed attacker trapped on the left side of the field against the touchline may shape the shoulders, hips, and lower body to give the impression of intending to pass the ball infield. In response, the defender often moves—perhaps only a foot's length (see figure 7.2), but this may be all that is required for the attacker to quickly change the position and route of the ball and go outside and beyond the defender (between the defender and the touchline). Similarly, when attackers approach a defender at speed, they may be able to put the defender off balance simply by shifting the ball a few inches (or centimeters) off the route on which it is traveling, then quickly shifting it once more to the other side, often with the same foot.

Figure 7.2 Show one side, go the other.

Another part of a great dribbler's makeup involves the ability to anticipate when and from where a challenge is likely to come. If the dribbler can predict and prepare for a challenge, along with any possible physical contact, then he or she gains the opportunity to choose and properly time the skill that is needed to eliminate the opponent. For example, if a challenge is likely to come from the side, with the players in close contact, the dribbler can lean into the opponent to remain balanced while moving with the ball. This is an advanced skill but one that will be increasingly necessary in congested areas of the field as attackers move with the ball and defenders chase them or recover alongside them.

The seize the moment drill (see page 139) encourages players to use these skills in order to be successful when surrounded by opponents before confronting them and escaping to make progress. Similarly, the directional-change dribbling drill (see page 140), an often-used practice, also challenges players to change feet, change direction, change speed, and make decisions quickly in response to rapidly evolving circumstances.

The art of dribbling is complemented by the art of running with the ball—that is, moving quickly into space with the ball, either to gain ground or to move away from opponents without the aim of deliberately attacking or confronting them. Running with the ball is commonly featured in counterattacking play. Upon regaining possession of the ball, the player must quickly assess the available options and decide whether running with the ball is the most appropriate choice. If so, then the player should follow through on this early decision by pushing the ball forward into the vacant space ahead.

In this maneuver, a player is in effect passing to himself, and the amount of touch needed on the ball depends on the space available, the proximity of any defenders who might challenge for the ball, and the player's own speed across the ground. All other things being equal, a bigger space ahead means that the first touch moving forward can be longer. This longer touch enables the attacker to build forward momentum because acceleration is not hindered by slowing to make unnecessary contacts with the ball. The player can take less strides before the next touch on the ball.

While on the move, the player must continue to make judgments about the direction that he or she should take, the length of the next touch, and which part of either foot to use. The player should also assess options for the next play, which could be either to release the ball or to run farther with it while monitoring the location and intentions of both defenders and fellow attackers. In order to negotiate these ever-changing circumstances, the attacker also needs to adjust stride length while running with the ball. If the attacker decides to release the ball, he or she must do so with precision and control while moving at optimum speed. The release may be made with either foot and any surface, so of course these skills must be practiced as part of the player's ongoing development.

It is also possible that a player running with the ball may be required to beat an opponent alone. In this case, the player will need to use the principles and skills of dribbling discussed in this chapter. A player who dribbles past an opponent may then need to follow up with strong and direct running with the ball.

In essence, dribbling is about control and calculation. The dribbler must control the ball and move with it under control toward spaces or players, which makes it crucial to know how much space is available around the opponent. The dribbler must also calculate when to move the position of the ball, how close to get to an opponent before making the crucial touch to get past, and how strong a touch is needed after a change of speed at the appropriate time. Feints may also be of use.

As the game continues to evolve at the higher levels, almost every player will need to learn the art of eliminating an opponent while moving with the ball. Midfield players in today's game are already required to be effective dribblers who can manipulate the ball under pressure to either protect the ball, move it into a position to release it, or attack and put an opponent off balance. Attacking fullbacks will also be required to attack defenders in wide areas, especially around the penalty box, in order to provide passes or crosses for others. And of course defenders will venture forward into midfield areas, where they may also be required to eliminate opponents, either alone or in combination play.

Strikers also need the ability to go it alone when faced with an opponent in or around the penalty area. Putting an opponent off balance when facing the goal can open up a space to one side and give the attacker the opportunity to shoot for a goal early in the knowledge that the defender may possibly recover and apply pressure. However, if the striker can eliminate the defender alone with good dribbling skills, then the defender may not recover, thus leaving the striker free to strike at goal or carry the ball nearer to goal before deciding how to finish.

And finally, it's worth noting that dribbling is also complemented by the art of eliminating an opponent without dribbling! For instance with the ball arriving and an opponent moving into a position from which he or she can be challenged, an intelligent player will, if the circumstances are right, allow the ball to run past or across the defender without touching it—and therefore eliminate the defender. For this ploy to work, the speed of the incoming pass must be suitable in that if it is not controlled by the receiver, it does not run out of play or to an opponent before the attacking player can first contact the ball. In addition, the receiving player must possess the ability to conceal his or her intention of leaving the ball and allowing it to run.

This maneuver can be performed anywhere on the pitch, with the ball arriving at any angle, and it is frequently used in the middle and attacking thirds of the field. It can, of course, be used in the defending third as teams pass the ball there but any miscalculation by the receiving player can be risky, lead to an interception, and allow the opponents to counterattack quickly over a short distance to the goal. When receiving a pass from a fullback or midfield player, wide attackers (see figure 6.2 on page 121) who are close to the touchline, with a marking opponent a few yards (or meters) infield, often act as if they want to control the ball but then, at the last second, allow it to run through their legs or across their feet. They then move quickly after the ball, which is running into space and away from the defender. Success here depends on two keys: the ability to hide one's real intention and the speed of the attacker to move toward the ball after it has been allowed to run.

DRIBBLING DRILLS

In the preceding discussion, we have examined the essence of dribbling, as well as the skills and decision-making qualities required for success. The practice activities referred to in that discussion are presented here. Coaches need to devise challenging dribbling practices in multiple forms, including ball manipulation practice, opposed practice, and game practice. The practices described here can be varied in many ways. In addition, any gamelike practice or man-to-man practice provides good opportunities for players to use dribbling and for coaches to teach and encourage this crucial art.

Congested Dribbling

Purpose

Dribbling the ball

Organization

Set up a circle that is 10 yards (or meters) in diameter. Position six pairs of players around the circle, as shown in the diagram, some 5 to 10 yards from the perimeter. In each pair, the partner farthest from the circle has a ball.

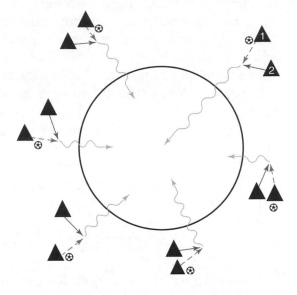

Procedure

1. Pairs of players outside the circle work together. For example:
   1. Player 1 passes to player 2, who moves at an angle to receive the pass.
   2. Player 2 then runs with the ball into the circle and attempts to cross the circle by evading other players with a ball who are also crossing the circle.
   3. After moving through the congested circle successfully, the player in possession passes the ball to a free outside player who carries the ball across the circle and is replaced by the passer of the ball.
   4. The skill is repeated moving in perhaps a different direction across the circle.

Coaching Points

- Upon receiving a pass, turn quickly with the first touch and place the ball into position for running at the circle.
- When carrying the ball, keep the head up, with the eyes maintaining a view of, but not fixed on, the ball.
- Detect and navigate the space available for carrying the ball through the circle.
- Change speed, direction, and strength of touch on the ball as required.
- Avoid others in the circle before accelerating out of the circle and passing to an outside player.

Variation

Extend the practice by employing a defender or two inside the circle, as well as two players who assist the dribblers inside the circle as needed (for example, to combine for wall passes).

Seize the Moment

Purpose

Dribbling the ball

Organization

Set up an area that is 6 yards (or meters) square. Position one attacker inside the area and one defender on three of the end lines. The coach is positioned outside of the area with a ball.

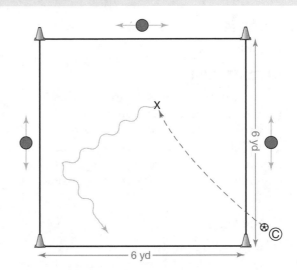

Procedure

1. The coach initiates play by feeding the ball to the attacker.

2. The attacker tries to break out over any available end line.

3. The three defenders are free to move around the outside of the square to prevent the attacker from escaping.

Coaching Points

- Deceive defenders by using clever and accurate ball manipulation skills and feints.

- Be aware of the defenders' movements and available spaces through which to break out of the area.

- Use subtle and varying touches on the ball when manipulating it and pushing it ahead on the final breakout movement.

Directional-Change Dribbling

Purpose

Dribbling the ball

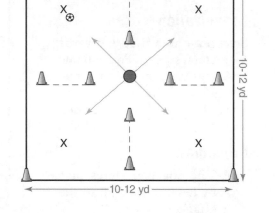

Organization

Set up an area that is 10 to 12 yards (or meters) square. Position four small (3-yard) goals as shown in the diagram. One of the four attackers has a ball and the one defender plays against whichever attacker has possession of the ball.

Procedure

1. To start the practice, the coach feeds a ball to one of the attacking players.

2. The attacker with the ball tries to dribble through one of the small goals before releasing the ball to another attacker.

3. The defender tries to prevent the dribbler from succeeding by pressing the ball or cutting off a route through the goal.

Coaching Points

- When in possession of the ball, change direction and speed.
- Manipulate the ball to deceive the defender.
- Feint as if intending to move in one direction before moving in a different direction to escape the defender or travel through a goal.
- Consider using one feint followed quickly by another to put the defender completely off balance.
- Always know where the defender is as you move with the ball, even though your focus may be on the ball and the surrounding area.

Goal Scoring

The art of goal scoring involves multiple key factors: moving into a goal-scoring position, reading the play, anticipating a striking opportunity, being aware of individual playing circumstances, and of course selecting and performing the method of accurately striking at goal. Scoring also requires players to possess ambition, desire, and optimism; indeed, these psychological features are found in the vast majority of "scoring predators." In addition, of course, top scorers must possess the physical qualities of agility, acceleration, speed of movement, strength, and flexibility. The world's outstanding strikers are also quick in various other ways—in their thinking; in their decision making; in moving as needed; and in using their head, their body, and, particularly, their lower limbs and feet when striking at goal. Perhaps this is why the world's leading goal-scorers score at the rate of around one goal per game played. Added to this outstanding feature of their play, they also contribute to the scoring records of others in that they supply them with opportunities to score by clever movement which attracts defenders to follow them and leave space for others to exploit.

In and around the goal-scoring areas, attackers are likely to be very tightly marked on numerous occasions, closely marked on others, and unmarked if they are lucky! They often receive passes or crosses or move quickly to a loose ball in the box, which requires them to adopt unusual body positions. This range of necessary actions requires a striker to be capable of moving in any direction and at varying speeds, often accompanied by an opponent. The actual strike at goal is frequently taken at a "stretch," or in an unbalanced position—and often when some form of physical contact is being made by the defender. To handle these various factors effectively, scorers must often be able to make either an early or a last-second decision about how to contact the ball accurately and, when possible, with optimum composure.

Of course, all goal scorers must develop the ability to escape defenders when necessary, which requires them to understand the playing circumstances.

Specifically, in losing opponents, the striker needs to be fully aware of the marker's location, capabilities, and likely actions. Therefore, strikers need to develop a good sense of how defenders think and tend to operate. Understanding these factors, as well as the orientation of the rest of the defense, helps strikers make good decisions about where and when to escape. They must also understand the situation of the player with the ball, as well as their own personal capabilities in terms of speed, change of speed, agility, and ability to time a movement.

Strikers must also be aware not only of spaces into which they might escape but also who else might move into those locations. Often, when a player is trying to lose a marker, the race to the ball is won by a change of speed combined with a change of direction. But it is crucial to know just when to change direction and how to alter the speed of movement. Players can learn these key elements of attacking play by engaging in simple man-marking games.

SCORING CONSIDERATIONS

Understanding the context and circumstances in which goal-scorers operate is central to the design of practice situations for strikers and others and is also crucial for the coach to comprehend. Regular practice in a variety of practice situations with varied service, challenges, and intelligent technical and tactical input from the coach will be vital if the young and developing striker is to progress. Varied degrees of time and opposition interference should be inherent in the practices that are offered to the player if his scoring skills and instincts are to be progressed.

When moving into a goal-scoring positions, the striker needs to consider how, where, and when the ball will arrive. For instance, when a wide player beats an opponent and moves into a crossing position in the final 20 yards (or meters) of the pitch, that development should alert any striker that the ball could be crossed in front of the goal. The striker can find clues about what is likely to happen by reading and recognizing the situation, both "on the ball" and in the immediate scoring areas, and by reading the movement and shape of the wide player's body.

In this game situation, the striker then has a choice to make: Move positively, quickly, and early into a profitable scoring area (for example, around the near post)? Or wait, read the early flight of the cross, and then attack the ball in flight? The striker may even have to respond to a secondary scoring opportunity resulting from a strike by another player. In making such decisions, the striker must be aware of the movements of other players, including attackers, defenders, and the goalkeeper. With these considerations in mind, coaches can use the random finishing drill (see page

147) to help forward players develop their ability to strike at goal when well placed to do so—and to react to shots by other players that rebound from the goalkeeper's saves or are deflected into their path. Also, this practice gives the strikers the opportunity to combine their play in order to score a goal. Wall-passes, overlaps and sequences of perhaps one- and two-touch quick passes enable the players to produce a striking opportunity.

Nearly 90 percent of all goals are scored within about 20 yards (or meters) of the goal especially in central areas. Knowing this, coaches should spend time educating strikers on how to move into, move within, and strike at goal from this crucial area. In making runs to make contact with the ball in these scoring positions, players who change speed and direction can increase their chance of success by eliminating any marking defender or one who is marking a space and notices the attacker's movement into a threatening area. Indeed, simply running and changing speeds can upset a marking defender's balance and momentum. Similarly, veering (at a late stage) from one running line to another can cause problems for a marking or tracking defender or even one who is awaiting the arrival of a striker into the goal-scoring area while observing the play.

Figure 8.1 illustrates a situation in which a striker who changes speed and direction upon moving into a scoring position may well get free from the opponent's attention. The movements by attacker 10 and attacker 9, though different, can both cause a defender to be surprised, off balance, and rendered slow to recover into the appropriate marking position. While the change of direction and speed are important, the timing is equally so, and the striker often has the advantage in that he is in a position to see the defender, the ball, and the goal as he makes these runs to make contact.

In figure 8.1, midfield attacker 4 feeds a pass to wide attacker 7 who attacks defender 3 and moves to a crossing position. As this happens, striker 9 ascertains the best route into a striking position, when marked by defender 5. Changes of speed and direction by attacker 9 may be needed to free him from a close and accurate marker like defender 5. Timing the movement into the goal-scoring position

Figure 8.1 Clever striker's movement.

and understanding the positions and movements of other players is vital in choosing the foremost position to attack.

In a crowded area in the penalty box, a striker with the ball at his feet must sense the opportunity for a strike at goal. Even when closely marked from behind, an excellent striker with the ball at (or arriving at) his feet will create a chance to shoot. The opportunity could be created by the player's ability to turn quickly and perhaps add a feint movement preceding the turn. When performed at speed, the feint may not only surprise the defender but also put him or her off balance and give the striker enough space to turn and strike at goal. Indeed, strikers need to develop the special skill of creating a scoring opportunity with little space and time because of close-marking defenders.

When facing an opponent in a goal-scoring position, top-class scorers can also use a quick but well-timed and well-weighted foot movement onto the ball in order to change its position before making an early contact. In fact, shifting the ball slightly and then contacting it instantly afterward (often with minimal backlift) is frequently a deciding factor in producing a strike at goal.

In order to develop this "close to goal" scoring skill, players should practice in congested areas in front of the goal where time and space are at a premium and opposition is included and appropriately-challenged to prevent shots at goal. Practicing in these circumstances also helps players develop the ability to threaten to shoot or feint to strike at goal before immediately shifting the ball to a more favorable position to strike. The crowded penalty box is a common feature in today's game, and the ability to operate at speed close to the goal will be a prime requirement for any high-class striker in the future.

Another crucial factor involves "slowing down" the mind. Top players can perform at high speed while remaining calm, controlled, and even relaxed during the act. These qualities can be developed only through repetitive practice and play. As the player develops the necessary shooting skills, along with confidence in his or her ability to strike at goal in various highly pressured situations, this familiarity with success is likely to calm the mind and enhance the player's control.

Of course, strikers also use instinct and intuition, and they frequently have only minimal (if any) time for thinking rationally about a playing situation, because often it all happens at high speed, and considered decision making is therefore almost impossible. Yet somehow, in some way, the striker is able to produce a successful strike at goal. Could it be the result of daily practice and of learning how to cope and produce shots under all conditions?

In contrast to the hectic nature of congested scoring situations, scoring in a one-on-one situation with a goalkeeper can seem to take forever in a player's mind, especially if considerable distance exists between the goalkeeper and the player as he or she moves onto the ball behind a defense. While moving at speed to stay ahead of recovering defenders, the player in possession must have the presence of mind to read the situation clearly—to anticipate and understand the goalkeeper's actions, to know what recovering defenders are likely to do, and to select how best to beat the goalkeeper—all while retaining mastery over his or her touches on the ball! Players can develop these skills by using a simple practice such as goalkeeper 1v1 (page 148).

The first decision for the attacker who is free to attack the goalkeeper is likely to address whether to strike at goal early even though moving at high speed. If the goalkeeper ventures too far forward from the goal, leaving an area that can be exploited, then a confident attacking player with the capability and confidence may choose to take that opportunity. If, on the other hand, the goalkeeper is canny and does not offer this option, then the striker must decide how far and how fast to travel with the ball before making the ultimate decision about how to eliminate the goalkeeper with the attempt to score.

As the striker goes through this decision-making process, it is likely that recovering defenders are reducing the distance between themselves and the player in possession and the goal. Therefore, the striker's decision-making process should include checking the situation visually to be aware of such developments including knowing where exactly the defender is and what his likely actions will be. Movement with the ball across the recovering defender can reduce the defender's options as the possibility of challenging for the ball while closing up on the attacker from behind can result in physical contact and the award of either a free-kick or penalty. Once in a scoring position, the crucial decision involves calculating whether to take the ball around the goalkeeper, to the side of the goalkeeper, or place it past or over him or her, as well as knowing just how and when to do so. The striker can also use a feint to cause the goalkeeper further problems in deciding exactly what to do. For example, one clever ploy that players can learn is feinting to pass the ball past the goalkeeper, then, at the last second, taking the ball to one side usually in the opposite direction from the feinted pass and across or around the goalkeeper before striking at goal.

In fact, the player in possession can even take the ball close to the goalkeeper *as if* intending to commit him or her before taking it to one side and around. Then, instead, the striker can either lift the ball over, if the goalkeeper "spreads" and goes to ground, or make a simple pass under the goalkeeper's body and sometimes between his or her feet. Breaking at goal (see page 149) is a simple practice that helps players develop this ability to break toward the goal and determine the scoring options. It is the simplest form of 1v1 scoring practice when moving at speed. The practice can be intensified by adding a time limit for making an attempt at goal; to develop it even further, recovering defenders from different angles and distances can be introduced.

In addition, the scoring goals drill (see page 150) helps players work toward developing just about every facet of finishing—shooting from distance, using combination play before striking at goal, scoring from short and long crosses, and cultivating the predatory instinct to rebound every strike at goal if not attempting to score personally.

As explained earlier, world-class strikers score at the rate of about a goal a game. Performing at such a level requires players to develop the capability to strike at goal from various positions in various circumstances and to use any part of the body to propel the ball toward the goal. Doing so requires players to regularly practice both conventional and unusual scoring skills. The practices explained in this chapter provide the basis on which other scoring practices can be developed and enhanced. Variety in service into the strikers, differing shapes and sizes of the practice areas, novel challenges for the players and a competitiveness all should be considered when taking these practices further and stretching the capabilities of goal scorers.

SCORING DRILLS

The activities referenced previously provide a catalyst for designing other scoring drills. It is important for the coach to keep in mind that a significant majority is scored with the player having had only one or tow touches on the ball from the central area of the penlty box. Designing drills with this in mind is crucial, and the coach will, of course, devise drills to suit and challenge the capabilities of the players. Scoring goals is an exciting and enjoyable practice, especially if competition is introduced. The competition can be between individual players, teams, or groups of players and, of course, against previous personal achievements. Scoring goals is the prime tactical objective of attacking play, and those prolific goal-scorers are possibly the most important assets that a team has. So regular and varied practice is vital and should be undertaken daily—especially for those who are primarily responsible for scoring.

Random Finishing

Purpose

Goal scoring

Organization

Set up an area that measures 18 yards (or meters) by 20 yards in front of a goal. Form two teams of three players each and position a goalkeeper in the goal. The coach is outside the area with a supply of balls.

Procedure

1. The coach feeds any type of service into the area (simple ground pass, volley, hand-delivered ball with spin, or service with a bounce).

2. Each team tries to be first to the ball and to either produce an immediate strike at goal or use combination play to produce a strike at goal.

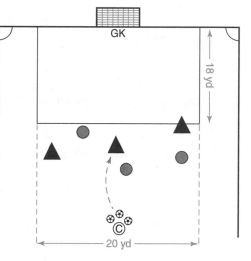

Coaching Points

- Expect any kind of service to any part of the playing area.

- Once the service is delivered, move early and quickly to the ball.

- Make appropriate playing and scoring decisions based on the service of the ball, the receiving position, and the location of other players and the goalkeeper. Options include striking at goal immediately, supplying a teammate with an opportunity to strike at goal, securing and protecting the ball to produce a strike at goal, or using combination play to produce a strike at goal.

- Use one-touch finishes to score, if appropriate.

- Place the ball past the goalkeeper with appropriate force.

- Keep strikes at goal low; if shooting from an angle, shoot across the goalkeeper to the far side of the goal.

- Rebound all shots from any player shooting on goal.

Goalkeeper 1v1

Purpose

Playing 1v1 with the goalkeeper

Organization

As shown, set up two areas that are each 10 yards (or meters) square and are located 15 yards in front of the penalty area. Position three attackers and one defender in each area and a goalkeeper in the goal. Each group of players will play against one defender, but another defender will be resting and will replace the first defender after the attack on the goal. A coach is outside each area with a supply of balls.

Procedure

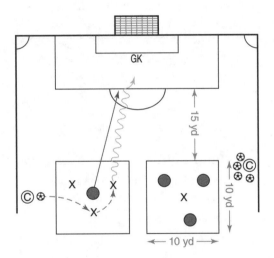

1. One of the coaches serves a ball into play, and the three attackers try to keep the ball for five passes, after which one attacker can leave the area.

2. The now-free attacker runs with the ball out of the area and tries to score while being chased by the defender.

3. Players in the other area rest until the currently playing group strikes at goal. Thus the groups alternate playing and resting.

Coaching Points

• If the player receives the fifth or subsequent pass, the player should use the first touch to move the ball toward the goal unless this is not possible, in which case, pass the ball again.

• A "big touch" is safe, since it takes the ball farther away from the chasing defender.

• When running with the ball, lift the head to observe the goalkeeper's action and the defender's position when recovering toward goal.

• Observe the goalkeeper's position to decide the best option for scoring—for example, lift or "chip" the ball over the goalkeeper and into the goal; shoot to the side of the goalkeeper if he or she is positioned poorly, thus leaving too much space on either side; or continue to run with the ball toward the goalkeeper and possibly pass it past or dribble around him or her while always being aware of the chasing defender's position.

Breaking at Goal

Purpose
Goal scoring

Organization
In an area located 30 yards (or meters) from the edge of the penalty box, position two teams of six to eight players each as shown. Position one goalkeeper in the goal and another waiting next to the goal. Each player has a ball.

Procedure
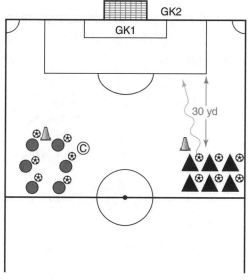

1. On the coach's command, the first player runs with the ball at the goal and attempts to score in a 1v1 situation against the goalkeeper.

2. As soon as the strike on goal has been made, the next player from the same team runs at the goal to score.

3. The team has 60 seconds to score as many goals as possible before the opposing team takes its turn.

4. The first goalkeeper operates for 30 seconds before being replaced by the second goalkeeper.

Coaching Points
- Run at a controlled speed with the ball over the distance to the goal.
- While moving toward the goal, observe the goalkeeper's positioning and actions.
- Make intelligent decisions about how to beat the goalkeeper—for example, shoot early; pass from a shorter distance past the goalkeeper; or attack the goalkeeper and score from short range with a pass or dribble around him or her.
- Incorporate the element of deception. For instance, when passing the ball past the goalkeeper, arrange the body, hips, and feet as if to pass past the goalkeeper's left side and then, just before the moment of contact on the ball, change the angle of the foot and pass to the goalkeeper's right. The same skill can be used when dribbling around the goalkeeper.

Scoring Goals

Purpose

Providing a variety of scoring circumstances

Organization

Set up an area that measures 36 yards (or meters) by 44 yards and divide it into two halves with four corner zones as shown. Position a portable goal at each end. Position two groups of six players each inside the area (four attackers and two opposition defenders in each half of the area). Also position a winger in each corner zone. Position a goalkeeper in each goal and a supply of balls behind each goal. One goalkeeper starts with a ball.

Procedure

1. The goalkeeper with the ball feeds it to the attacking team in the nearest half of the playing area.

2. Four attackers can shoot from distance but initially cannot leave their own half. The other two attackers operate in only the attacking half.

3. Attackers can take shots from long distance or pass to one of the two attackers in the attacking half to produce a shot. The defenders in each half are active as soon as the goalkeeper releases the ball to start the practice.

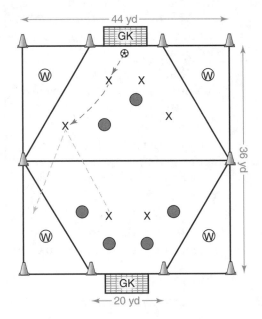

4. As the practice develops, the wide players can receive passes in their zones and either shoot or provide service to other players on their team.

5. Any wide player can receive a pass and feed other wide players before providing a service to the attacking players.

Coaching Points

- In the 4v2 situations in each half, attacking players can shoot from distance and should generally try to keep shots low and accurate. However, various situations will arise that may enable them to score over or around the goalkeeper from distance.

- Deciding which scoring skill to use should depend heavily on being aware of the goalkeeper's position either before or after the first controlling touch and also the actions and presence of opponents.

- Attackers in the attacking half "rebound" all long shots at goal.

- The four attacking players under pressure from the two opponents in their defending half can either feed the ball to their two attacking players in the attacking half to produce a strike at goal or pass to the wide players in their zones to produce a cross or short pass for a strike at goal.

- As the practice progresses, a player in possession of the ball in the defending half may run with the ball into the attacking half and either produce a strike at goal or provide another player with the chance to do so.

- Wide players (wingers) in possession in their area can either cross the ball, run with the ball and then cross or pass to an attacker around the goal, or run with the ball into a central area and supply another attacker with a shooting opportunity.

- The same drill can be done with fewer players by playing 3v1 in each half of the field but in a reduced area. With younger players, the area should be modified to suit their needs.

chapter

Counterattacking

One tactic that has always been productive in attacking soccer is the counterattack. When a team regains possession of the ball in any area of the pitch, a counterattack can be fruitful if the ball is moved quickly and accurately toward the opponent's attacking third of the field in order to produce a strike at goal. In fact, counterattacking can account for a considerable percentage of a team's goals. In the 2004–2005 season, for example, Premier League champion Chelsea scored 42 percent of its goals in this way.

As part of a counterattacking tactic, some teams defend deep in order to entice the opponent to come toward their goal. Since many attacking teams involve defenders in their attack and also concede space behind and between the rear defenders, they can be vulnerable to a counterattack. The largest source of counterattacking goals stem from regaining possession in central areas of a team's defending half of the pitch when the opposition has committed some defenders to the attack and their team is fragmented (a factor in designing relevant coaching sessions for this aspect of the game.)

Counterattacking takes various forms. Some teams counterattack quickly after regaining possession by delivering long passes to or for attacking players moving behind the opponent's central defensive areas or to the sides of the defense for a strike at goal. Other counterattacks involve rapid shorter-passing sequences of one- or two-touch contacts that move the play forward quickly into a striking position.

At their best, for example, Arsenal and Barcelona, within their style of play, have moved the ball at speed from their defending third into a goal-scoring position in no time at all by having players receive and release the ball with minimal touches. Indeed, these teams have moved from defending third positions to attacking third positions in as few as 10 seconds before producing a strike at goal, often by means of either one- and two-touch passes or quick and dynamic runs with the ball.

There are also other ways to counterattack. One team-based tactic involves pressuring the opponent in possession in its own defending and midfield areas in order to regain possession while already close to a position from which to strike at goal. Another approach involves solo play. Here, a player who regains possession of the ball, especially if alone, carries it forward at speed, eliminates defenders as necessary, and produces a strike at goal.

KEYS TO SUCCESSFUL COUNTERATTACKING

The commonly accepted principles that underlie counterattacking play are as follows: regain possession of the ball; move the ball forward as early as possible, either by running with it or by passing it; have players who recognize the countering possibility and provide passing outlets around or ahead of the ball; and use a quick attack to produce a strike at the opponent's goal while maintaining defensive security. These principles should guide practice design and serve as the focus of counterattacking mentality.

Counterattacking can be initiated by intercepting a pass cleanly, which requires that players develop their defensive ability to read, interpret, and anticipate an opponent's attacking play. Observing an opponent in possession of the ball, as well as other nearby opponents who may serve as pass receivers, is a defensive skill that should be nurtured in young developing defenders and in a team's overall defensive play. Defenders can find clues about a passer's intent by looking closely at the position of the ball at the passer's feet, how the passer addresses the ball before contact, and the shaping of his or her hips and upper body.

In addition, players who observe the degree and angle of pressure exerted by the defense on the ball holder can anticipate the direction, type, and timing of likely pass options. Once the pass is made, the defender must then observe its speed and direction, along with the movements made by the opponent (if any) that he or she is marking, in order to be first to the ball and intercept the pass.

Intercept the pass and counterattack (see page 162) is a simple practice that helps players learn to read a play and intercept passes. Specifically, defenders in this practice observe the two players in possession, forecast when a pass may be released, and develop their skill at intercepting passes and, when possible, counterattacking.

Although anticipation is important, defenders also need to be clever and avoid moving too early to a pass that they think could be intercepted. As discussed in other chapters, intelligent attacking players can send false signals to defenders before releasing the pass or change their intended passing target at the last second.

Once the defender has considered all relevant factors, success depends largely on his or her ability to accelerate quickly, if needed, in order to move to the ball. At the same time, the defender must also understand that the opponent may also move to the ball and use his or her body, especially if receiving the ball with his or her bck to the defender, to block the defender's route to the pass as it travels. Thus two important mantras for defenders are "win the race to the ball" and "expect contact from the opponent on arrival at the ball."

As the defender travels to intercept the ball, he or she should see and assess the situation, both ahead and around. Then, upon taking possession, if possible, he or she should either immediately release a one- or two-touch pass to a teammate or run with the ball into space or across a recovering opponent. Thus the ability to travel with the ball at speed, alone or while being pursued, is an important skill in the modern game. Players can develop this ability through the simple practice presented in the interception drill (see page 163).

Even if a defender is unable to intercept a pass cleanly and initiate a counterattack, another option may still be available. The defender may be able to make contact with the ball a split second before the opponent does, deflecting the ball or pushing it away from the intended receiver and toward a teammate who can then start a counterattack. This action is often referred to as "spoiling" possession for the opponent, and it can indeed be effective in defensive play.

At the same time, implementing it often requires the defender to go to ground and to reach for the ball to make contact. Defenders need to be careful in this skill as making physical contact with the opponent could result in a free kick against the team. However, fair and well-timed contact with an opponent and the ball is allowed and should be taught as a defending skill. Once the spoiling has taken place, the defender must recover his or her balance and defending position in order to rejoin the play as quickly as possible.

Whether a player is releasing the pass immediately after regaining possession or passing the ball while running at speed, accuracy is vital. In fact, many counterattacks are stalled by inaccurate passes (other reasons include failing to escape from opponents in pursuit of attacks ahead of the ball and straying into offside positions). Because defenders are likely to drop toward their own goal to secure the central attacking areas, attackers must be able to pass accurately through the defense and between defenders.

Figure 9.1 illustrates the likely defensive structure when a team concedes possession of the ball in a midfield area during an attack. Counterattacking quickly in this scenario embodies the various factors that we have considered so far. Speedy recognition of the chance to counterattack is needed from attacker 10, as well as an effective first touch of the ball—whether it be a controlling touch before the next passing contact or a first-touch pass for attacker 9.

Meanwhile, attacker 9 needs to time and route his or her run according to the positions and movements of defenders 5 and 6, who are likely to drop quickly toward their own goal once their team loses possession. As a striker, attacker 9 should always be expecting his or her team to regain possession and should therefore be ready to serve as a willing outlet for the counterattack—either receiving the ball in front of defenders 5 and 6 or,

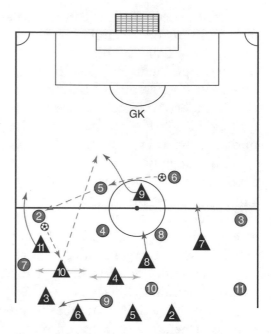

Figure 9.1 Regaining possession of the ball.

preferably, moving to receive behind the defense.

When releasing the pass to initiate the counterattack, if that is the best option, attacker 10 must be mindful of both the necessary pass speed and the possible presence of the goalkeeper in a central position who could intercept the delivery. This threat may require attacker 10 to apply backspin on the ball and angle the pass into the run of attacker 9 and away from the goalkeeper.

Other players also need to recognize the chance to counterattack, even before attacker 10 releases the pass. They should assume a counterattacking mind-set and move forward to support attacker 9 as required. Attackers 7, 8, and 11 should move forward early and at speed to offer support for attacker 9, and players behind or around attacker 10 should also move forward to supplement the counterattack while maintaining defensive security.

If attacker 9 is not favorably positioned for an early pass, then attacker 10 may decide, upon taking possession of the ball, to run with it. If so, he must assess multiple factors: the positions of defenders (such as defender 4) who could apply pressure, the possible pass options in the circumstances, and whether it is within his or her capability to dribble and eliminate defender 4, who may apply the pressure.

In some cases, quick pressure applied by the opposition may prevent the player who takes possession from either passing or running the ball forward. In order to deny this pressure, the player may need to play a wall pass to eliminate the pressing opponent. Alternatively, the player may direct the play away from the area where possession was regained and into a less populated area of the pitch from which, if possible, the counterattack will be continued.

If, on the other hand, the counterattack gains momentum quickly, attackers ahead of the ball need to know the positions and movements both of opponents and of supporting attackers. These players must move into appropriate support positions, and, upon receiving the ball, move forward. This means that they must be capable of directing the ball with the first touch, preferably into a position that enables the team to continue moving the play toward the opponent's attacking third and especially at the goal. Therefore, these players need to be capable not only of passing the ball at speed but also of receiving it at speed and directing it as needed to keep the play progressing quickly forward. Forward players also need to understand that they can move to attract defenders in order to open up opportunities for others to receive passes in better circumstances.

Preparing the counterattack (see page 164) is a small-sided game in which a team defends deep in its own half, leaving only one player to defend in the attacking half. Upon regaining possession, the team may be able to initiate a quick counterattack using the principles we have been exploring.

After the initial regaining of possession and the quick release of the first pass, other players must support the counterattack. Midfielders and fullbacks may be able to advance at speed while observing other players' positions as they move into support or goal-scoring positions, though not all of them should go at the same time—or should they?!

Defenders on the counterattacking team should also move forward. Doing so enables them to compact the play so that the whole team supports the counterattack while also ensuring that the defense is organized in case the opponent immediately replies to the counterattack. Defensive security also requires the counterattacking team to be careful not to commit too many players to goal-scoring and high-supporting positions.

The final phase of the attack is crucial, and the success of a quick counterattack depends on taking up receiving positions ahead of the ball. Attacking players must understand the movements needed to receive a pass, but if defenders mark and track well, then attacking players may use runs and other movements for different reasons. For example, a striker who is well marked might make movements or take up a position that defenders must cover in order to open up opportunities for other attackers to exploit. In this way, players moving forward in a counterattack should understand both their own and other players' circumstances—and understand the kinds of movement to which defenders must react.

Figure 9.2 shows movement by striker 9 away from the central areas with the understanding that a defender must counter this movement. The maneuver opens up an opportunity for wide attacker 7 to move centrally at pace to become a receiver in the newly created open space and possibly strike at goal.

Here is the context of the move: Upon regaining possession of the ball, attacker 10 has carried it forward at speed while being pursued by recovering defender 8. Attacker 9 has moved to a position on the blind side of defender 6, knowing that defender 6 must track this movement. Thus attacker 9 has both become a threat to receive a pass from attacker 10 and moved defender 6 away from a central support position. Attacker 7 breaks toward the infield from a flank position and is now able to exploit the space created by attacker 9's movement.

Figure 9.2 Clever striker movements.

The aim of this final phase of the counterattack is to supply the ball to a player in a goal-scoring position by means of either a cross or a pass to a teammate. Such a pass or cross is usually delivered while moving at speed and must be precise in order to help the possible scorer. On some occasions, of course, the delivering player faces severe pressure from an opponent and must release the pass or cross instantly. The aim, however, is to supply others with the most accurate delivery possible under the circumstances.

Since it is highly likely that the finishing skill will require minimal touches, players should regularly practice diving headers, sliding contacts, and side-footed strikes at goal from within the final 18 yards of the central areas of the pitch—within the penalty area. They should also practice handling situations in which one attacker is opposed by only the goalkeeper.

If the opponents recover quickly into positions between the ball and their goal—and it is not possible to provide service for or produce an early strike at goal from the counterattack—then the attacking team must now build an attack in order to score. Support is crucial for this slower type of attack, so the supporting midfield players who joined the initial counterattack remain important in this later phase, but in a different way. The team must now change its strategy and mind-set in order to find a way of penetrating a deep and often well-staffed defense.

Doing so is likely to involve passing the ball accurately and with speed, as appropriate, around the first bank of defenders and often across the pitch. This tactic requires quick, accurate passes, usually to the feet rather than to space, while players ahead of the ball seek receiving positions inside the defensive structure.

Against a deep and well-organized defense, the attacking team may have to move the ball laterally across the field to the open side—or, referring back to our example, to attacker 7 (see figure 9.3). Passes should be quick, using no more than two touches where possible, and usually to a player's feet. In the example, attacker 8 has noticed, before receiving the ball, that a space exists between defenders 8

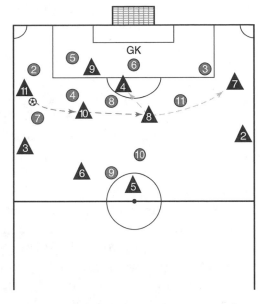

Figure 9.3 Creating a scoring opportunity off a delayed counterattack.

and 11 through which the ball can be passed to attacker 10 or 9.

Quick, precise passes cause problems for defenders by requiring them to respond at speed to the movement of the ball across the front of their penalty box. Some defenders act quickly, whereas others hesitate and move more slowly, and attacking midfield players need to recognize the resulting gaps exposed in the defending structure and take the opportunity to service attackers in the penalty box. Indeed, they should be looking for such defensive errors continuously while the attacking team is in possession in the attacking areas. More generally, scanning the defensive structure is a prime skill for any attacking player at any time.

Returning to our example, this type of scanning means that, in anticipation of receiving the ball, attacker 8 already knows the defensive organization before the release of the pass. Once the pass is made, to either attacker 10 or 9, clever attacking play can be initiated by using combination play or individual skills to produce a strike on goal.

Once the quick-passing sequence is under way and attackers are searching for receiving positions within the defending block, players in possession of the ball can often succeed by using either a disguised pass or an obvious but fast pass to an attacker within the defense. As discussed in the chapters about passing and receiving (chapters 5 and 6), attacking players need to be capable of disguising their intentions and deceiving defenders both when they are in possession of the ball and when they are not. An attacker who gives little if any clue about the intended direction of a pass can catch a defender expecting something else and thus confuse his or her decision making.

If a fast ground pass is delivered to an attacker's feet inside or around the edges of the penalty box, then other players nearby must support the receiver for possible combination play in the heart of the defense. This effort may lead to either a strike at goal or a pass to another attacker for a strike at goal. Passing to and then joining in with a central attacker often produces a strike at goal. As an alternative, the receiving player within the defensive block may turn quickly—perhaps with a disguised action or a clever unexpected turn—and shoot at goal. Of course, a well-crafted aerial pass to a tall player may also be used to produce the strike at goal.

Thus either combination play or individual cleverness may enable the attacking team to penetrate *through* the defense, and a well-crafted and measured aerial pass may enable the team to penetrate *over* it. Given these various options, coaches must help players develop their understanding of and competence in exploiting a back line. Players should regularly practice the high-level skill of supplying the final pass to the goal scorer against a congested defense. Along with attacking centrally and penetrating a deep defense, many goals are scored by crossing the ball. Around 30 percent of a team's goals will be from crosses into the penalty area. So specifically practicing this aspect of the game will pay off either during a counterattack or from building a goal from a stalled counterattack.

Figure 9.4 shows a typical circumstance found in today's game. Opponents drop to a position deep in their attacking half and position nine or ten players between the ball and the goal. Penetrating that block of players is a challenge, and the attacking team must often use cleverness, subtlety, and deception—both on and off the ball—to unlock the block and produce a strike at goal.

So, if the counterattack phase is foiled, then the attacking team shifts to a strategy of "building" a goal. Attacking quickly has always been and will continue to be a significant and productive tactic, but penetrating a deep, well-organized defense poses

Figure 9.4 Operating against a deep defense.

very different challenges. Here, the attacking play is slower, less direct, and focused on penetrating a congested area of the pitch rather than an expansive one.

Even so, similarities do exist, including the need for fast and accurate passes to an attacker (where appropriate), accurate and well-directed first touches, and fast action within the penalty area in order to create a strike at goal. Regular practice of this aspect of attacking play enlightens players as to the possibilities and the variations they can use.

Building a goal will be a regular challenge for teams that base their attacking play on shorter-range passing and playing through the thirds of the field. Generally, the more a team passes the ball square and backward as it attacks, the more likely the defense is to drop toward its own penalty area and set up a block of defenders. Penetrating a block of defenders is and will continue to be a challenge for attacking teams.

With all of this in mind, players should regularly practice counterattacking at speed—a vital and rewarding phase of play—while also recognizing that if a quick counterattack is not possible, the alternative is to build a goal.

COUNTERATTACKING DRILLS

This section presents practices that help players develop their counterattacking skills. These practices are intended to serve as catalysts for thought, and coaches are encouraged to expand the ideas in order to devise effective counterattacking practices for their players. Such practices should involve regaining possession from opponents as a prelude to the act of counterattacking.

Intercept the Pass and Counterattack

Purpose

Intercepting passes and counterattacking

Organization

Set up an area that measures 20 yards (or meters) by 8 yards and divide it into three zones as shown in the diagram. Set up two small goals at each end with cones for a total of four goals. Position two attackers in each end zone and one defender in the middle zone. One attacker has a ball.

Procedure

1. To initiate play, either the defender passes a ball to one of the two attacking pairs or the coach serves a ball to one of the pairs or one attacker may pass to the other in the same zone.

2. The two attackers who receive the ball try to transfer it to the attackers in the opposite end zone by passing it, below head height, past the defender in the middle zone.

3. The defender, who is free to operate anywhere in the middle zone, tries to intercept the attackers' passes.

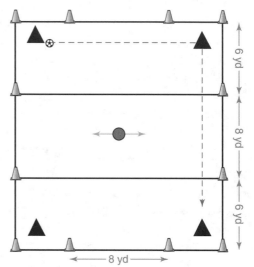

4. Upon gaining possession, the defender runs with the ball and tries to either pass through one of the small goals or run over the end line with the ball.

Coaching Points

- Read the intent of the player in possession.

- In response to lateral passes, slide or shift sideways with the feet apart, the knees bent, and the upper body leaning forward.

- Move quickly—usually laterally—to intercept passes and even slide or go to the ground to intercept the ball or deflect it away from its intended receiver.

- Upon contacting the ball, move it forward as early as possible by running it at the opponents and through a goal or over the end line.

Variations

- Use two defenders in the middle zone.

- Increase the area's width to 10 or 12 yards (or meters).

Interception

Purpose

Intercepting passes

Organization

Set up four cones 25 yards (or meters) apart and four additional cones 5 yards outside of the first four. As shown in the diagram, position two attackers at each cone and (optionally) two target players in the middle area. One attacker has a ball.

Procedure

1. Attacker 1 runs with the ball for about 15 yards (or meters) before passing to attacker 2 with pace. The cones marking the corners of the square are 25 yards (or meters) apart.

2. Attacker 3 anticipates the pass to attacker 2 and steps forward to intercept it. Attacker 2 now replaces attacker 3, and attacker 1 becomes attacker 2.

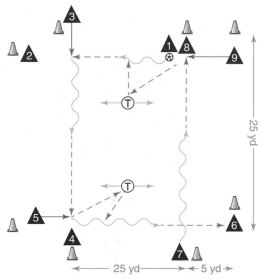

3. If target players are included in the practice, they help the intercepting player by acting as possible receivers of his or her one-touch pass after the interception (or wall pass if the intercepting player runs with the ball).

4. Attacker 3 runs about 15 yards (or meters) before passing to attacker 4.

5. Attacker 5 anticipates the pass and steps forward to intercept it.

6. Attacker 4 now replaces attacker 5, and attacker 3 becomes attacker 4.

7. Play continues in this manner.

Coaching Points

- Anticipate the pass release by the player running with the ball.
- Upon intercepting a pass, the first contact is vital and should be pushed well ahead of the feet in order to cover ground quickly, or the first touch should be used to pass to target players who then return the pass to the running player.
- When running with the ball, keep the head up and the eyes able to see the position and movement of the ball and other players.
- Release passes off of either foot using various surfaces to contact the ball.

Preparing the Counterattack

Purpose

Defending to counterattack

Organization

Set up an area that measures 70 yards (or meters) by 45 yards and divide it into two halves. Position a goal at each end. Form two teams of equal number (8v8 or 9v9), including goalkeepers. Teams occupy their respective halves as if a kickoff was taken to start the game.

Procedure

1. The game is started by the coach, who serves the ball to either of the goalkeepers who initiates an attack for his team.

2. Upon losing possession after an attack, a team is allowed only one defender in the attacking half of the area; the attacking team can have an unlimited number of players in the area.

3. The defending team drops into its own defending half, tries to regain possession, and, if successful, attacks from its position.

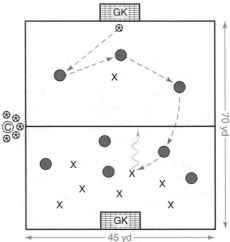

4. After a goal, the game commences with another kickoff or the coach feeds the ball to the goalkeeper on the team that scored.

Coaching Points

- The one defender in the attacking half is unlikely to succeed at pressing the opponent's possession and thus drops toward the half line, cutting off passes into the central areas, then assumes an appropriate position and prepares to participate as an outlet for a pass from a deep regain of possession.

- The defenders in the defending half mark press the ball and move together as the ball is passed across and around the defensive structure.

- From their marking and covering positions, defenders should read the play and try to intercept passes and otherwise spoil the opponent's possession.

- Upon any type of possession regain, defenders should try to progress the play quickly and early by using forward passes or moving forward with the ball as appropriate.

- If a counterattack cannot be initiated, the team should build a goal through accurate passing sequences that progress the play into a scoring position.

Defending

As the game continues to evolve, defenders will need to evolve as well. The game is becoming quicker, more technically expansive, and more tactically liberal because teams are changing their systems of play from game to game—and even within games. In response to these changes, defenders must equip themselves with the athletic, technical, and tactical resources to anticipate, match, and counter the actions taken by attackers.

In order to succeed, defenders need to be capable not only of generally "reading the game" in all phases but also of specifically reading an immediate opponent's intention. They must also be able to anticipate the likely outcome of a given playing situation and prepare their body to move in response to an attacker's play. In short, defenders who learn how to position themselves tactically, ready themselves in terms of balance and foot and body position, and read the game intelligently will greatly enhance their ability to defend against an opponent's attack.

DEFENSIVE SKILLS

Defending, following positioning correctly, and having an awareness and understanding of events taking place will be followed by the core skills of defending. Being in the right place at the right time as a defender is a prelude to the actual defensive decision-making of whether to mark, press, track, cover, or execute some other defensive responsibility. Every defending event is different, but the key to effectiveness is for the defender to first position himself correctly. One crucial defensive skill is the ability to mark an opponent or an important space. When defending against an immediate opponent, success depends on the ability to intercept passes, "spoil" passes that travel to the opponent, and to prevent the receiver from turning with the ball and gaining momentum should he receive possession.

To spoil a pass, the defender makes contact with the ball as it arrives at an opponent's feet when he has his back to the defender, for example, and, if unable to intercept and take possession of the ball, force it out of the opponent's possession by causing it to run away from his immediate reach. Doing so may require the defender to go to ground to make the challenge, but it can also be achieved with the defender remaining on his or her feet and marking closely as the ball arrives. Spoiling frequently takes place with the ball arriving at the opponent's feet. But, if completed legally, it can be used to deflect or destroy passes that arrive at any height.

Defenders must use the linked skills of understanding the likely intentions of the player in possession of the ball and at the same time seeing and understanding the activity of an immediate opponent. Indeed, the hallmark of an excellent defender is the ability to anticipate what will happen as the attacking play develops and then quickly change as needed from one defensive function to another. The very best defenders define their defending role and responsibilities based on multiple factors: their understanding of the game's defensive principles, their understanding of the current threat to the goal, and of course their personal defensive capabilities as well as those of the immediate opponent and the defending context.

Despite the importance of these cognitive aspects, I cannot recall the last time I observed a coach teaching defending players how to read the game, especially the player in possession of the ball—to notice the feet and hip position of the player, to recognize his or her exaggerated feints and attempts at disguise, to watch his or her head and eye focus and relate them to the actions of other attacking players. Of course, the implied message here for attacking players is to avoid showing your intention whenever possible!

A defenders' ability to read the developing game situation—and, particularly, the opponent's intent—can, in a sense, put them one step ahead of attacking players. It certainly enables defenders to make quicker decisions and take quicker defensive actions; in other words, it enables defenders to be more proactive than reactive. More specifically, defenders who clearly see the picture painted by the attacking team's actions can be wiser and quicker in organizing their feet, body, and mind for effective tactical defense.

Another defensive skill that should be learned by all players is that of pressing the ball. Pressing involves moving into a position two or three yards (or meters) away from the player in possession of the ball and on some occasions, slightly less. If performed at the right moment, pressing can reduce the time available for the player in possession to decide and act as he or she wishes. Specifically, it can reduce the player's passing options, reduce his or her operating space and time, and reduce his or her technical and tactical possibilities.

Defenders must also be able to recognize when there is a need to press, which requires the ability to observe the developing play and understand what defensive action is called for. A defender who does move to press should be clear about two things: (1) his or her intent in pressing—for example, using his or her specific approach angle and foot and body positioning to allow the opponent certain playing options and prevent others, and (2) the location of other attackers and defenders and their current involvement in the action. These two pieces of knowledge enable the defender to understand whether help is likely to arrive or whether he or she must defend alone in this particular circumstance.

In order to press the ball effectively, of course, the defender needs the physical capabilities of both acceleration and deceleration. He or she must also be able to balance correctly and ready the feet before pushing off strongly to engage the receiving player or the player in possession of the ball.

Once in position to press, the defender must be able to shift balance, move the feet quickly while remaining balanced, and change speed and direction to deprive the opponent of certain options. To this end, the defender should be able to lead with either the left or the right foot, regardless of his or her personal preference for one or the other. Of course, there will also be occasions when a defender shows the opponent neither left-side nor right-side options, and that is an art in itself!

Once in a pressing position, great defenders can quickly shift their body position to move from one pressing angle to another. This can create confusion in the mind of the opponent and force him to change his decision and options often within a split second. If the attacking player is troubled by this changing of position, then the pressing defender can often move closer to the player in possession and increase pressure, forcing him to turn away or even back toward his own goal.

Defenders also need to be able to turn quickly through varied angles and at varied speeds, and this ability will only become more necessary as attacking players continue to pass and interpass quickly when close to goal and also in midfield areas. This type of attack requires defenders to be capable of shifting their body weight and their feet at high speed in a variety of directions while also thinking about how to manage the unfolding situation, especially in congested areas.

Press the ball (see page 172) is a simple and effective practice that helps players develop their ability to press, mark, and track opponents. If one player presses the ball, others (if not supporting the pressing player) will have other responsibilities. They may be required to mark a space, track a run, or mark an opponent.

As discussed earlier, it is crucial for defenders to understand the principles of marking an opponent. Significantly, distances are of importance and will affect marking positions. The defender who has the responsibility to mark an opponent must be aware of his distance from his immediate opponent, his distance from the player in possession of the ball, the presence or otherwise of a covering defender, and the possibility of a more important threat from another attacking player. Another factor is the degree of pressure applied to the ball by any pressing player and the general flow and direction of the opponent's attacking play. As the play moves closer to the two opponents (attacker and marking defender) the distance between them is often, though not always, reduced—usually by the defender.

During match play—and, in fact, in any game or practice where defending is involved—the defender must at all times observe both the attacker's movements and the player who has possession of the ball, usually from a position that is inside (nearer to the central areas of the field) and goalside (between the attacker and the center of the goal.) This positioning is explained in figure 10.1. There are, however, occasions when an opponent is marked from a position nearer to a touchline than to the center of the field.

From any marking position, unless the defender is deliberately allowing the opponent to receive the ball, the defender needs to give himself or herself a chance of intercepting the pass or at least having the first touch of the ball—that is, spoiling! Creating this opportunity depends, of course, on the defender's distance from the attacker and on his or her ability to move quickly to the ball. Failing that, if the ball is passed successfully to the

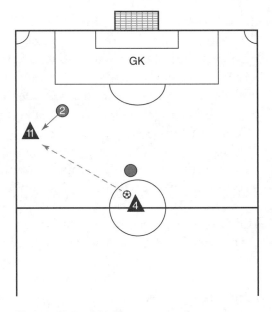

Figure 10.1 Marking opponents.

attacker, then the defender needs to be in a position to try to prevent him or her from turning with the ball—or, if the opponent has turned in possession, from gaining momentum if he or she chooses to run with the ball.

Many goals are scored because of either poor marking or a defender's inability to apply meaningful pressing skills to contain an opponent in possession of the ball and deprive him or her of preferred attacking options. All defenders must learn to mark, press and track with both the speed and the agility to counter the opponent's movements (whether with or without the ball). They must also know when to do so. Indeed, it should be second nature for defenders to speedily recognize their responsibility to press or mark a space or opponent, especially in deep defense in the defending third of the field and in the attackers' central approach-play areas. Players can develop crucial pressing, marking, tracking, and other defending skills through the man-marked passing drill presented earlier in the context of attacking (see page 106 in chapter 5).

Defenders also need the ability to accelerate in a variety of circumstances—for example, chasing or tracking attacking players over some 40 yards (or meters) during a counterattack, moving quickly over 15 yards to challenge for the ball as an attacker moves toward the goal, or accelerating at high speed over 5 yards to prevent an attacker from shooting in the penalty area. To develop overall athletic speed, defenders need to work on their agility, acceleration, and ability to run at high speed over distance, all underpinned by appropriate strength development.

The element of speed in defending applies not only to individual players but also to groups. For instance, a pair or group of defenders using coordinated movement must appreciate the appropriate speeds at which to move. Consider a 2v2 situation in the central areas of the pitch close to goal. Normally, one defender presses the attacker in possession of the ball while the other probably offers a degree of cover in a zonal defending structure. Once the ball switches from one attacker to the other, both defenders need to quickly change responsibilities by moving from a pressing role to a covering role or vice versa. Doing so requires each defender to change balance and height and shift the feet quickly in order to push off with speed. Any delay gives the advantage to quick-thinking and quick-moving attackers.

Thus defenders must know and understand their various responsibilities involved in defense and recognize when and how to change roles. Furthermore, this knowledge and understanding should be an essential part of defenders' training and education about the game—especially how to do so when operating at high speed.

Team units must also use coordinated speed in order to succeed tactically. As opponents change the play across the field in midfield areas, the midfield defending unit, which uses zone defense, must "slide" across at the pace of the ball. Doing so is no easy task if the ball is passed at speed, and the defending unit must retain appropriate distances between its members in order to deter or intercept passes to forward players seeking to receive the ball behind the midfield unit.

In addition, some members of the midfield defending unit may have to quickly press the current ball holder while others position themselves appropriately in relation to this tactic. Therefore, defending players must move at speed not only laterally but also diagonally or vertically as the unit changes its shape on demand. The defensive mantra in this situation is "move together, stay together, and arrive together."

The same principles apply to the back line in a zonal setup. In order to defend efficiently, members of the unit must maintain effective distances from each other, from the goalkeeper, and from the defending midfield unit—all while monitoring their relationships with their opponent and using appropriate speed of movement.

Back-four slide and defend (see page 173) is a simple practice that helps players develop their ability to be part of a mobile back line that responds to movements of the ball across the field. To expand the practice, forward players can be added to the attacking team to link with a midfield unit that plays for the team in possession and move the ball around and across the field.

When defending zonally, the back line of defenders must be able to operate at speed as a coordinated unit. For example, when crosses or passes are delivered into the penalty box and cleared by defenders, the back line and other defenders can move quickly away from their goal, thus leaving attackers offside if the ball is immediately returned into the penalty box. Succeeding with this tactic requires defenders to recognize the chance to use it safely and assertively. If the ball is cleared over distance and beyond the reach of attacking players, then the defenders can move out away from goal and some of the defenders toward the ball.

It is important here for defenders to know the overall situation. As the unit moves forward, its members must know whether attackers are also coming out, where other opponents are located and where they are moving, and whether a fellow defender has been left behind. They must also decide whether to keep moving forward or stall the forward movement and reset the defensive line. Making this decision wisely requires them to be aware of the chance that the ball can be delivered into the penalty box again. While doing this, defenders must be aware of the actions of attackers around them. Some may quickly attempt to move to an onside position while others may be slow to move away from goal and be in offside positions. However, the real danger may arise from attackers who come from deep positions and attempt to move into scoring positions if their team regains possession from the ball that has been cleared. These attacking runs may be from central or wider areas so defenders should search for these threats from all directions when moving away from the goal and defend accordingly.

Thus, though it is important to move together at speed and retain defensive organization, the group's ability to do so depends on each player's ability to recognize the possibility for moving forward and compacting the defensive structure. This is all part of a player's ability to know and read the game, which of course must be practiced in training. Once again, the "move together, stay together, and arrive together" mantra should prevail, but of course not all defenders will start the move from an orderly defensive shape because of their defending position when the ball was first cleared.

In summary, the capability to read the game's events is crucial, and the world's best defenders are frequently one step ahead of attackers. They seem to possess an uncanny ability to know what will happen and to act on this knowledge before others do. This feature of defending, along with rapid decision making and speedy but controlled action, is crucial to defensive tactical effectiveness. At the same time, defenders must also develop athletic speed and agility for moving both toward the ball and against opponents with the ball. Players who lack these athletic qualities will be exposed by opponents at the highest levels of the game.

On the other hand, a player who develops these decision-making and athletic qualities, along with practiced and flexible defending skills, has a chance to be successful if also blessed with the psychological qualities needed by top defenders. These qualities include courage, concentration, resilience, discipline, and a will and desire to defend that develops into an *enjoyment* of the art of defending. They should be encouraged in all players involved in defending—be they forward, midfield, or defending players.

DEFENDING DRILLS

The concepts covered in this chapter, such as marking, tracking, and pressing, will develop with the use of the drills outlined here and, of course, by using other relevant drills. All players must understand the basics of defending, even the wide and central attackers who are frequently required to defend in their search for an attacking opening while their opponents retain ball possession. Naturally, defending skills and techniques must be woven into the team's defending strategy and tactics, but it is essential for all players to understand the team's tactical objectives and the skills required to be successful in those objectives.

Press the Ball

Purpose

Pressing the ball

Organization

Set up an area that measures 36 yards (or meters) by 20 yards with a 5-yard end zone at each end. Form teams of three; positioned behind each end line.

Procedure

1. The coach initiates play by serving a ball. Serves should vary, including both ground balls and aerial balls, going to different positions in the area, and sometimes favoring a team but other times being neutral.

2. Both teams of three enter the area and try to gain possession of the ball.

3. When in possession, a team tries to retain possession against the opponent and supply the ball to a player who can carry it into the end zone.

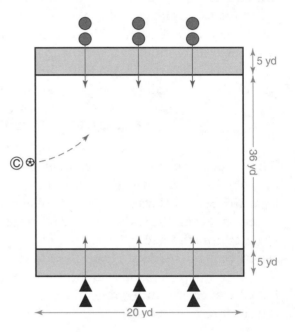

Coaching Points

- Be aware of who marks who when defending.
- Press the ball with the intention to show opponents to the infield or toward the touchline or sometimes in no exaggerated direction.
- When pressing, remain balanced and shift the feet quickly in response to any movement of the ball by the attacker.
- Seek the right moment to challenge for the ball and dispossess the player in possession.
- If not pressing the ball, mark opponents and track any forward runs.

Back-Four Slide and Defend

Purpose

Back-four sliding

Organization

Set up half of a regulation field and position two teams of four as shown in the diagram. Position a goalkeeper in the goal. One player on the team closest to the center line starts with the ball.

Procedure

1. The back four move the ball quickly from one side to the other (it is not essential that all four players receive the ball when transferring the ball from one side to the other).

2. Passes may be made using two touches and, in some instances, one touch.

3. In response, the other defending team of four should slide together as a unit, keeping their distances uniform and changing the shape of the line appropriately for the speed and direction of the passes being made.

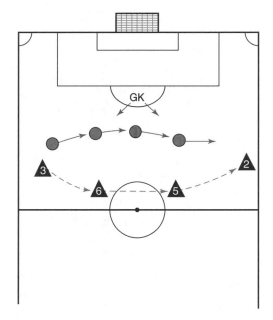

4. The goalkeeper must support and "sweep" the central area behind the back line. As the practice develops, he or she can also be involved in changing the ball across the field with the feet.

5. As an extension to the practice, both teams can have a goalkeeper who is involved in changing the play from one side to the other by receiving passes from a defender and passing to other defenders.

Coaching Points

- Be aware of the distance between each other when moving across the field in response to the movement of the ball.

- Observe and quickly respond to the direction of the developing play—laterally, diagonally, and horizontally—as the team in possession passes the ball.

- Know exactly where other members of the back four are positioned as the unit moves, and communicate when necessary to keep the required distances between the players.

- As the unit responds to the ball movement, work using the manta: move together, stay together, arrive together.

Variation

This practice can be extended by adding two midfield players who can operate for both teams and are involved in the transfer of the ball across the field. Also, the introduction of other midfield and forward players enables the coach to increase the challenge and the learning opportunities for the players.

Part III

Tactical Speed

chapter 11

Strategy and Tactics

The term *strategy* generally refers to the overall planning needed in order to achieve a goal. In soccer, the term *game strategy* refers to the planned series of events and circumstances that we thread together in order to achieve a victory or other goal. The elements of game strategy include temporal factors, as well as various defending and attacking approaches on the individual, group (unit), and team levels.

We also need to consider the means for implementing the game strategy—that is, the many parts, or workings, or ingredients, of the overall strategy. These elements are referred to as tactics. For instance, one possible individual tactic would be for a wide attacker to attack a fullback inside before going outside with the ball; one possible group or unit tactic would be for a back line to continuously push up quickly and condense the play; and one possible team tactic would be for a team to defend deep as the opponent attacks. In short, then, the strategy is the overall planning of the affair, and the tactics are the operational parts of that plan—in other words, what we want to do and how we will do it!

In order to succeed in soccer, defensive tactical objectives must be understood by all members of the team. For example, key considerations might include the following: when to apply pressure to the ball holder, how deep to drop before applying meaningful pressure, which players (if any) to mark on a man-to-man basis, and the required dimensions (from front to back and side to side) of the defending block. Such considerations are ingredients that we can use in designing our overall game strategy—how we will play in order to win, or at least not to lose.

Of course, game strategy also involves attacking tactics. For example, a team planning how to score might consider ways to start an attack from the goalkeeper's possession, movements by midfield players to position themselves to receive the ball from back players, movement by forwards to drop deep in order to receive passes from midfield players or alternatively attacking the spaces behind vulnerable center backs.

PLAYING STYLES

Different teams use different styles of play—that is, they have different ways of thinking about the game and, based on that thinking, different ways of making decisions about how to function. Playing styles are evident in the technical and tactical choices that players make and in the positioning and movements of players, both when a team is in possession of the ball and when it is not. A given team's style of play consists of such elements as its combined passing linkages, its choice of attacking probes, its decision-making priorities, and its answer to the opponent's playing method.

Some teams adhere strictly to their chosen way of playing regardless of the opponent or the current state of the game. Others are more flexible and may alter their style, for example by changing their player personnel, switching players between positions, or even changing their overall playing system. Playing style also depends on players' attitudes. Some coaches wish in general to play the game at high speed whether in or out of possession and this requires high levels of fitness, application, and commitment to that style of play. If one or two players cannot devote themselves to this style of play because of their reluctance to perhaps fully extend themselves athletically and psychologically then the proposed style of play will not be suitable and fruitful. Often, head coaches inherit players at a club when they take over the role from a previous coach and the first task is likely to be to profile players and examine their attitudes and receptivity to a certain style of play.

In addition, a team's playing style depends on the direction of play, its functional or expressive features, and the speed and intensity of play. For instance, upon gaining possession of the ball, a team might attack quickly—straight toward the opponent's goal—and might do so in part by using long forward or diagonal passes. If this approach is a regular, high-priority feature of the team's attacking strategy, then the team could be classified as a direct team. In other words, it tries to minimize the number of square or back passes and prefers to attack the opponent as early and as quickly as possible even if doing so risks a loss of possession. This type of team play will often result in passes delivered behind the opponent's defense, and these passes are supported quickly with the whole team pushing forward. This is done so the team can support the receiver of the pass or regain ball possession.

Take a look at figure 11.1. Upon receiving the ball, attacker 2 turns and delivers a long aerial pass toward the outer areas in the attacking third of the field. He does so knowing that striker 9 will recognize this option because of team practice sessions. As the pass is delivered directly into the wide areas, striker 9 breaks to the wide area and the midfield players 7, 4, 8 and 11 push forward quickly to immediately support striker 9 or support the build-up of play that he creates when gaining possession.

This tactic aims to bypass the opponent's midfield players and fullback 3. Defender 6 could be under severe pressure from striker 9 if he seeks to clear the ball or take possession of a poor pass and be pressed quickly by striker 9. Should defender 6 decide to head the ball while under pressure from striker 9, then attackers 2, 4, and 8 move forward quickly into areas they suspect the ball will drop. If defenders 3, 4, and 11 arrive in this area first, then they are immediately pressured by the players supporting the attack. If the forward pass is good and striker 9 takes possession, then

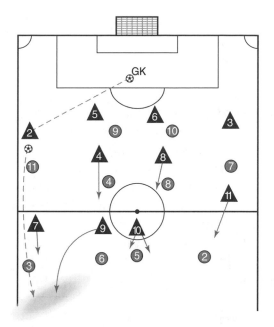

Figure 11.1 Direct attacking tactics.

the attacking players are well placed to support striker 9 and continue the attack. This is a typical direct team strategy whereby possession is put at risk but a regain of possession higher up the field through pressing tactics could be the result if the team is well-organized.

In contrast, another team might attack less directly and quickly. This team might prioritize retention of the ball as a prime tactic when moving the play toward the opponent's defending third. As a result, it will use more passes in order to progress—often made sideways and backward to avoid a heightened risk of losing possession.

A direct team, then, frequently attacks along the quickest, most penetrative route toward the goal, whereas an indirect team takes a route that is less well defined. Some teams, of course, fall somewhere in between—that is, somewhere along the direct–indirect continuum. These teams use both forward passes and side and square passes as major and distinguishing features in their approach play.

Some teams have a collective rather than individualistic manner of playing. These teams are characterized by simple, quick interpassing and often look well rehearsed in their attacking and defending play. Many South American teams, on the other hand, encourage and endorse individualism as part of their makeup. These teams encourage individual players to perform as they see fit, and in doing so their players often place the ball at risk. Indeed, individual cleverness and expression—sometimes leading to overindulgence—is welcomed.

Teams also play the game with different levels of intensity. Direct teams tend to be characterized by high intensity and speedy play, whereas indirect teams generally operate at a slower pace but with injections of high-intensity play when appropriate. Teams generally choose a style of play that fits their players' attributes, attitudes, and capabilities, their coaches' beliefs, and the playing culture of their nation or club. The choice of playing style may also be influenced by climate, the current state of the game, the presence of certain influential players, and the age of the team's players.

With all of these factors in play, a team that does not adopt a well-defined and well-understood playing style and philosophy may find that its recruitment and development of players becomes haphazard. It may also lead to confusion, a lack of understanding of playing objectives and fall into a random way of playing the game. In contrast, a well-defined playing style gives the team a basis on which it can formulate strategies and tactics at all levels—individual, group, and team.

As with overall strategy and tactics, defending tactics in particular emanate from a chosen method. For example, a team might choose to defend by pressing and marking all over the pitch whenever possible. Alternatively, it might choose to drop deeper before confronting players in possession of the ball, allowing the opposition to attack, with an eye toward persuading or even forcing the opponent to relinquish possession through good defensive positioning, organization, and compactness. The choice between defending earlier and defending later can be made on the basis of the following considerations.

- Perhaps the opposition, if pressed in its own defending half, will lose possession because its skill level is insufficient to retain the ball under severe and coordinated pressure.

- In some cases, the opposition starts its attacks by having the goalkeeper throw the ball to players in its defending third in order to establish a rhythm for possession play. In response, the defending team might choose the tactic of pressing the opponent in order to disrupt passing fluency and cause the opponent to start attacks in a different (unpreferred) way, such as having the goalkeeper kick the ball.

- Alternatively, if the opponent is highly skilled at retaining possession while advancing, the decision to press the ball all over the field might prove futile and exhausting, both physically and mentally. Instead, the defensive team might choose to drop to a position (say, 10 yards or meters) behind the halfway line with a compact team shape. This tactic could reduce high-intensity running when defending, reduce the space in which the opponent can operate, and reduce the distances between players and groups of players, thus making penetration less likely.

- If a team's back players lack speed and agility, then participating in an early and high-pressing defense could leave them exposed to the space behind the defense and unable to match the speed and movement of the opponent's attackers moving into that space to receive passes.

So, teams choose particular defensive strategies and tactics for a variety of reasons. It is difficult to counter a team that can morph from a deeper-defending approach to a high-pressing approach (and vice versa) within a single game. In fact, this kind of strategic and tactical flexibility will be increasingly required as the game continues to evolve. The following section explains some defending and attacking tactics that are currently in use and will become paramount in the future of the game.

DEFENDING AND ATTACKING TACTICS

Some teams base their strategy on the idea of playing at a speed that they think will disrupt the opponent, either when defending or attacking. For example, a team equipped with quick defenders who can accelerate rapidly and cover ground (say, 10 yards or meters) at high speed may gear its defensive play to quickly press an opponent who is either receiving or in possession of the ball. As the opposing players try to escape pressure by moving the ball to teammates, other defending players reapply the pressure quickly and relentlessly until possession is regained.

Such an approach is a team tactic that is understood and enforced by all players, and it continues until either the defending team wins possession or the opponent establishes composed possession that compels the defending team to regroup, possibly in a deeper-defending phase of play. Some teams, whose fitness level is high enough, use this pressuring tactic throughout the game. Others use it in a more selective and calculated manner. In either case, the intention is partly to prevent the opposition from gaining momentum to the attack or establishing dominance in possession and partly to test the opponent's will and technical ability to play at high speed.

Sustaining this pressuring tactic for the duration of a game is demanding in every sense. The continuous high-intensity movement and changes of direction can be fatiguing and erode a player's sharpness, both in and out of possession. As a result, some coaches work with their teams to recognize certain triggers or signals that activate the pressing tactic for a relatively short period of time. The cue might be, for example, an uncontrolled pass by the opponent, a square or risky pass to a teammate, a pass to a technically poor or nervous opponent with a defending player nearby, or a certain vulnerable passing circumstance (for example, a pass from a center back to a left back). The role of the coach here is to educate players to recognize such possibilities, both in practice and during game play. Some teams also use an early-pressing tactic for a period of time before dropping deeper toward their own goal to defend.

No matter when or where a team adopts a pressing tactic, it must do so through a controlled and high-intensity approach that is adopted by the entire team. If three players press the opponent urgently and early, but a fourth player does not recognize the situation or contribute to the effort, the tactic is likely to fail, thus allowing the opponent to escape the press. Figure 11.2 shows an example of faulty pressing in which four defenders press both the ball holder and possible outlet pass targets. In this example, attacker 6 has passed the ball to attacker 3. Immediately upon reading the pass to attacker 3, defender 7 applies pressure with help from defenders 2, 8, and 9. However, central defender 5 fails to mark striker 9, who drops to receive the ball. On receiving the ball under little or no pressure, attacker 9 can turn and attack the back line with a pass or decide to run with the ball centrally to commit opponents. Therefore, the team tactic of pressing the ball has failed here because of the poor defending of this one player.

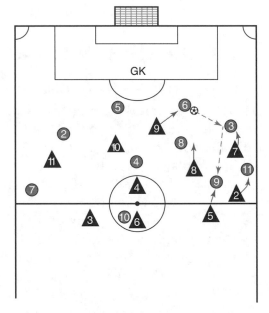

Figure 11.2 Poor execution of a pressing tactic.

In contrast, figure 11.3 shows an example of a full-team press where all defenders recognize and contribute to the full pressing tactic high up the field. Specifically, the defenders take up positions from which to deter, deny, or intercept passes to their immediate opponents and to press any receiver of a pass from fullback 2. In this example, the goalkeeper throws the ball to attacker 2, after which the following sequence immediately occurs.

1. Defender 11 presses attacker 2, who is about to receive possession of the ball.

2. Defender 9 cuts off the possible pass to the goalkeeper if necessary.

3. Defender 10 moves to prevent attacker 5 from receiving the ball (in some situations, defenders 9 and 10 could reverse their roles depending on the distance from each other and the likelihood of defender 5 or the goalkeeper becoming the next pass receiver).

4. Defender 7 moves centrally to discourage and even prevent a pass from attacker 2 to attacker 6.

5. All other defenders mark opponents in a position from which they can immediately apply pressure should their opponent receive a pass.

6. The goalkeeper for the defenders acts as a sweeper behind the back line.

In order to succeed, the defending team must be aware of the opportunity to press together, work assertively to influence passing options, defend vigor-

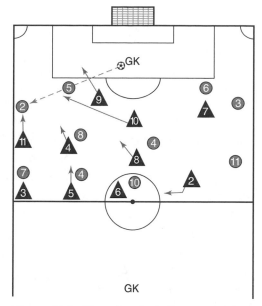

Figure 11.3 Pressing the ball successfully.

ously but under control in pressing anyone who receives the ball, and mark accurately those who don't. The team may agree on certain tactics—for example, that the ball holder should not be able to choose pass options at will but should instead be influenced to release passes only into certain areas or to certain players. The defending team will agree on those areas and chosen receivers when preparing for an upcoming competition and will practice implementing the tactic in training. In addition, the tactic may be adjusted as needed for different opponents.

The reverse is also sometimes true—that is, teams who usually choose to defend deeper, allowing the opponent to come to them, may suddenly change tactics and press quickly, early, and high up the pitch for a period of time. If players understand how to use a pressing tactic effectively, the tactic of pressing at different and unexpected periods in the game can surprise and disrupt the opponent.

A change of tempo and tactic can also be an effective ploy for an attacking team. The change may come in the form of a quick pass, a quick-passing sequence, a player accelerating quickly while carrying the ball, or players simply moving both themselves and the ball either more quickly or more slowly than before. For example, when facing a team that defends deeper (dropping, say, to the halfway line of the pitch before applying pressure) and cedes possession to the attacking team, the attacking team can pass the ball unopposed and perhaps even at a leisurely pace while moving the play forward. However, once the attacking team establishes possession around the halfway line, its passes may need to be moved more quickly to resist any pressure now being applied by the opponent. This increased pace may not reach the level of a high-speed sequence but still increases the tempo of the attacking play.

On the other hand, if a team wishes to change the play from one side of the pitch to the other in order to attack quickly on the weak side, then its passes are best delivered early and quickly, using only one or two touches when traveling across a midfield unit of players. If these passes are accurate, the attacking team can supply an attacker (perhaps in a flank position) with a pass that provides more time to control the ball and either choose the best pass option or personally drive forward with the ball. Passes made when using this tactic move more quickly than the opponents can move over the same distance, thus giving the attacking team an advantage.

Figure 11.4 shows a team changing the play quickly from the left-side to the right-side wide attackers. In this example, the attack is constructed on one side of the field. Attacker 8 receives a pass from attacker 3 and quickly and accurately changes the direction of the attack to supply either attacker 2 or attacker 7 with a long pass to expose the space on the opponent's weak side. Passes from attackers 3 and 8 (and from attacker 8 to the weak-side receiver) need to be delivered accurately, with speed, and if possible to the space ahead of the intended receiver (attacker 7 or attacker 2). The

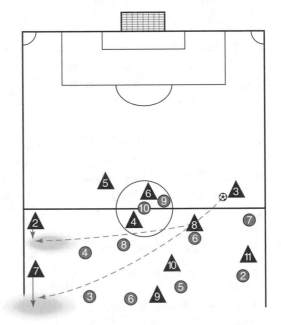

Figure 11.4 Changing the speed and direction of passing movements.

ability to turn quickly on receiving the ball in order to switch the play will be an important integral factor in the success of this passing sequence.

Similarly, once a team establishes possession in the opponent's half of the field, with many defenders located between the ball and the goal, the team's ability to move the ball across and around defenders is vital as it searches for a pass that centrally penetrates the defense. The attacking team will be helped by moving the ball accurately and quickly, and the final pass to a player in a goal-scoring or goal-making circumstance may well have to be the speediest pass in the sequence. The defenders will try to press the ball holder and reduce the space between themselves—that is, remain compact—so that passes targeted at these spaces are threatened with an interception. As a result, the attacking team may need, for example, to deliver a pass to a forward's feet inside the penalty box with high speed and with no evidence that the pass is about to be delivered.

In fact, passing at high speed and with disguise can be highly successful in the attacking third of the field against a compact defense. This action often triggers a sequence of quick interpassing between attacking players using minimal touches—one or two—which is difficult and at times impossible for defenders to react to and counter. Thus speed overall, and change of speed in particular, are vital tactics to use during the approach toward an opponent's goal in today's game, and this will continue to be the case in the future.

Just as teams vary their passing and possession tempo, individual players who serve as possible passing targets vary their own movement speeds. For instance, as play develops toward the attacking third of the field, or even deeper toward the opponent's penalty area, intelligent attackers know how to vary the speed at which they offer themselves as pass receivers. For example, an attacker may start at a slow pace and then explode and run at high speed to receive the ball, thus catching the defender unawares. Any such burst, accompanied by a fake or dummy movement before the change of speed, can earn the forward both time and space in which to operate when receiving the ball in what could be high-pressure circumstances.

So, we see that clever teams and players can slow the pace of a passing sequence in order to outwit defenders but then suddenly speeding up the play to gain the advantage. Similarly, teams or groups of players can also pass at high speed to "kill off" any pressure being applied before slowing down to a speed that better suits their chosen attacking tempo. Teams that recognize the opportunity to counterattack quickly will pass and move at high speed, but if they are unsuccessful in creating the final breakthrough from the quick attack, they will slow down to retain possession and build a scoring opportunity at a reduced tempo.

Different teams play the game with different intentions. Some try, when in possession, to play at high intensity for as long as possible and rarely change their game tempo. Others play at a slower speed and are perhaps more deliberate and controlled in their game style. Each team, of course, should employ tactics and tempos that generally suit it. Even when trailing in the latter stages of a game, for example, teams that employ a slower tempo do not necessarily adopt a more direct and long-passing style to increase their chances of producing a goal-scoring opportunity. Instead, they are more likely to increase the speed at which they employ their preferred game style. Specifically, their passes between players are quicker, their runs are likely to be more explosive, and their passing sequences are speedier. This increase in the speed of play is more common than resorting to a more direct playing style.

Such speed variations are often employed by South American teams. Colombia, for instance, possesses the capability in its approach play to attack in an almost leisurely manner when speed is not paramount. However, they (as is the case with more teams in the modern game) also possess the capability to suddenly play at high speed in their attacking half and around and inside the penalty box. Often, this is done in response to a defender's positioning error, an ill-timed press attempt, or the availability of space in which to run with the ball at speed (albeit over a short distance) to commit a defender or attack a space.

An increase in the speed of attacking play may also be triggered by a sudden and explosive movement by a forward or midfield player who attacks the space behind the defense. As teams today defend deep—with probably 10 defenders in or around the penalty area, in addition to the goalkeeper—it is vital for attackers to recognize when to increase the tempo of play and be able to do so effectively.

When an attacking team uses "same-paced" playing methods, defenders become familiar (and to a certain degree comfortable) with the mode of attack, and their bodies and brains adjust to the necessities of operating at that speed. But rapid changes of playing speed—and rapid changes of movement speed within that larger variation—can surprise defenders. Along with directional changes, these variations in tactical speed can cause defenders great discomfort and often dislocate the defensive structure. Such tactics severely test a defender's ability to rapidly decide what to do, change direction and speed, and select the proper defensive skill to use. Indeed, such demands often exceed a defender's capability; in other words, defenders often fail to respond and act quickly enough when attackers use such tactics and skills.

Whether defending or attacking, individual players and teams can gain a tactical advantage if they possess the capability to vary the speed at which they operate. To do so, they must be able to recognize when and how to change playing speed in order to create the surprise element—in both individual and team tactics—that "catches out" the opponent. Coaches can devise practices to help players develop the ability to change speed rapidly, particularly when attacking, as illustrated in change of tempo (page 187).

STRATEGY AND TACTICS DRILL

Following is a drill that can be used to explain and develop the ideas offered in this chapter.

Change of Tempo

Purpose
Change of playing tempo

Organization
Set up an area that measures 18 yards (or meters) by 46 yards with two 18-yard end zones and a 10-yard central zone. Position four attackers and two defenders in the starting end zone, two defenders in the middle zone, and three attackers in the other end zone. One attacker in the starting end zone has a ball.

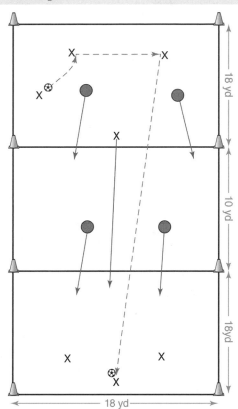

Procedure
- The four attackers in the starting end zone try to keep the ball away from the two defenders for six consecutive passes.
- Once the six passes have been made, the ball is moved over the middle zone, past the two defenders in the middle zone, and into the other end zone. Should the two defenders take possession, their challenge is to run with the ball out of the playing area as quickly as possible with the coach immediately serving another ball to the four attackers to commence a further attempt at combining play for six passes before changing the play.
- As the ball is transferred to the other end zone, the two defenders in the middle zone and one attacker from the starting end zone join the group of attackers in the other end zone.
- The two defenders in the starting end zone now take a position in the middle zone.
- Play continues in this manner.

Coaching Points
- Retain possession by assuming good support positions, executing simple passes, and often slowing the play down.
- After achieving the target of six consecutive passes, switch the play quickly to the other end of the playing area.
- Quickly support the receiving unit by sending one of the initial attackers to join them, thus creating a 4v2 situation in that end zone.
- Deliver the pass to the other end at speed—usually in the form of a lofted, driven pass to allow more time for the receiving unit to control and pass the ball before the two defenders from the middle zone arrive and exert pressure.

Developing Soccer Intelligence

"He's an intelligent player." "He's not tactically aware." You've probably heard such comments during your time in soccer. What exactly do people mean when they say these things? One suspects that they are referring to the player's game understanding and decision-making capacity. But what makes a player tactically aware? How does one become a better decision maker?

IMPORTANCE OF DECISION MAKING

Players make decisions largely based on perception and awareness of what is happening around them. Decisions can also be made through various processes—conscious reasoning, intuition, emotion, and sometimes instinct. Conscious reasoning helps us consider the facts of a situation, what action to take, and how and when to take it. However, this process can take considerable time, and it may not always be available to a soccer player involved in a high-speed game. Even so, players do sometimes have the opportunity to consider which course of action to take and then act accordingly. Some players choose an easy and safe option from a range of alternatives and are satisfied with that. Others try to choose the most effective option in the circumstances, both for themselves and for their team.

Players can open up good possibilities—and become more valuable to their team—if, in addition to possessing a wide range of skills, they also develop their understanding of the principles of play, the various circumstances that may arise, and the capabilities of individual players. The game rarely presents exactly identical situations, especially in free play, but players benefit from understanding key general criteria for good decision making in various circumstances. Key criteria for making good decisions when attacking include the location on the field of play, the positions of opposing players, likely ball possession situations, actual and likely support movements, and recognition and understanding of possibilities for gaining an advantage. Similarly, defenders must be able to consider their own key criteria, including their location, their reading of the player in possession of the ball and other defenders involved in the play, and their understanding of the unit's or team's defensive priorities.

While it may help at a given time for a coach to simply tell a player to "do this" or "do that," this approach does not necessarily help the young player learn about key decision-making criteria or develop an effective process for making successful decisions as circumstances change during the game. Instead of simply giving orders, coaches must help players make sense of the play in order to help them develop their decision-making skill. Meeting this challenge depends on the coach's depth of knowledge and understanding of both the game and the player! The key to helping players develop their decision making is not to rigidly prescribe what to do but rather to help players develop a flexible thinking process based on certain criteria and on good understanding of a range of playing situations.

Players' decisions may be influenced by various factors, including the team's chosen tactics and style of play, the state of the game (for example, leading or trailing, available time remaining, or playing with or against 10 opponents), the coach's instructions, and (to a great degree) their own and others' competencies and attributes. Decision making can also be affected by incentives offered by the coach and the immediate playing circumstance. In addition, players can be affected by an internal "feel" for the situation. For example, a player's decision might be affected by emotional factors—such as fear, anxiety, or a desire for self-protection—if he or she is confused, unsure of what to do, feeling overwhelmed, concerned about taking a risk that might concede possession, or sensing that an opponent might intercept a pass, which could lead to criticism from the coach or others.

A player's history and personal experiences also play a crucial role in his or her decision making. For example, recalling past events and outcomes from practice or game play can help a player anticipate, read a situation, and make a correct decision. The player may well recognize the intentions of an immediate opponent or support players or recognize patterns of activity and remember past successful decisions in similar circumstances.

There are many implications here for coaches. What type of practice should be designed to help players learn to make correct tactical decisions with or without the aid of the coach? Tactical decisions involve the player in making a judgment and executing a maneuver, perhaps to take advantage of a game scenario or counter an opponent's advantage. For sure, the ultimate testing ground for tactical decision making lies in the game itself, but this ability can be facilitated through carefully considered opposed-practice situations based on the capabilities, understanding, and experiences of the players involved.

Of course, other types of practice can be used to familiarize players with likely patterns of movement and possible ideas for solving the challenges. In other words, practice does not need to be fully opposed with equal numbers every time. The art of the coach lies in knowing which type of practice will best help a particular group of players learn a particular playing concept at that time—custom-made practice!

Repetition in practice, though not always identical, helps players quickly identify signals, patterns, and likely outcomes. This is especially true if the coach guides players (where needed) toward the crucial factors to observe and analyze as they are making decisions. In fact, however, few coaches teach players what to observe when playing, either in practice or in a game. For example, as an opponent prepares to strike the ball, should the defending player look at the opponent's head, hips, or upper-body position—or attend to some other factor—in order to forecast what will happen? So, in order to become better decision makers, players need repetition, rehearsal, guidance from the coach, relevant experience, and familiarity with game situations (possibly through practices designed by the coach).

All of this, however, is insufficient. Players must also understand their own capabilities and attributes. Know thyself! A player who lacks understanding of his or her proficient technical range may be overambitious, which can result in poor decision making. In such cases, the coach's knowledge and guidance are particularly important. One of the coach's pivotal roles is that of extending a player's range of technical competence while enhancing the player's understanding of and confidence in his or her abilities in the context of the game's attacking and defending principles. Players also need to understand the competencies of other players—both teammates and opponents—in order to know, for example, which pass to deliver to which player at which time and how.

FACTORS IN DECISION MAKING

The key to successful decision making is to prioritize the available alternatives. For example, a defender must decide whether to mark the immediate or designated opponent or leave that player and collect, say, a midfield runner to the back of the defense. This one decision involves numerous factors.

- Can the ball be delivered to the runner, or does pressure on the ball close off that option?

- Is the runner being tracked by one of the defender's teammates? If not, can any other defender collect the runner?

- If the runner continues at the same pace, will he or she likely move into an offside position when the pass is delivered?

- Can I (the defender) afford to leave my immediate opponent to collect the runner, or would my immediate opponent then be likely to receive a pass in a dangerous position?

For further exploration, let's look at figure 12.1. In this example, attacker 3 is in possession of the ball in the attacking midfield area, and attacker 8 has made a forward run to the back of the defense. How does defender 5 make a correct defensive decision? Should he or she continue to mark attacker 9 as a possible receiver of a pass from attacker 3, or leave attacker 9 and take responsibility for covering the forward? What would you do, and why?

The defending player needs to understand not only the principles of defending but also his or her team's chosen tactics. Learning to be an intelligent decision maker requires that the defender understand the general risk involved in various possible actions and the implications of his or her specific actions. Taking a step back, does the

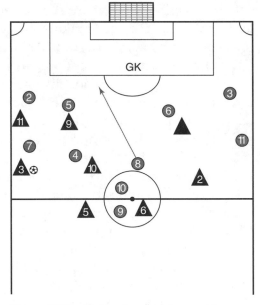

Figure 12.1 Defensive decision making.

coach understand the factors involved in making good decisions, and can he or she devise tailored practices to help players learn to make the right decision? Furthermore, can the coach explain, teach, and clearly advise players in the decision-making process? As in all tactical practice design, the following questions should guide the coach's design process.

- What do I want to introduce or improve?
- Why am I working toward this goal?
- When does this happen in the game?
- Where does this happen in the game?

- Who should be involved in the practice?
- How do I start and end the practice?

So, what, why, when, where, who, and how? These are the guiding questions for designing tactical practices, whether for a small group of players or for the entire team. For instance, a coach might design a practice specifically to help a fullback and a wide attacker combine their defending efforts against a tactic that the next opponent is known to use (see tactical decision making, page 197). Perhaps the wide attacker who will be opposing our fullback continually moves infield to receive a pass from the center back 5. Upon receiving the ball, this wide attacker frequently turns with the ball and attacks the defense by either running with the ball or passing it forward. In addition, at the same time that the wide attacker moves infield, the attacking fullback moves forward into an attacking position. These are tactics that we need to negate! Here are some key questions to consider.

- What should our wide attacker and defending fullback do to counter the opponent's expected tactic?
- How should the coach explain (if necessary) how to make this decision?
- If the opposing wide attacker does move infield and the fullback does advance, what factors should be involved in making the correct decision about how to defend?
- Should the defenders stay man-to-man with their opponent, or should they stay within their areas or zones? In other words, what should they do, and how do they decide?
- How might the decision be affected by factors such as the timing of the opponents' movements, clear communication between the defenders, and the defenders' distance from each other as the opponents move?

It is crucial here for the coach to do several things: design a practice that is specifically relevant to this particular opposition tactic, locate the practice in the areas where it is likely to be employed, and understand the key criteria that will help the defending players make the correct decision. Tactical decision making (page 197) explains possible practice features that could be used by the coach. This is a simple practice involving only seven players, and it can be organized to operate on both sides of the pitch so that the right-sided fullback and wide attacker can also use this practice.

It is true that players learn many things simply by playing the game. However, they are likely to be helped even more by practice that is directed and specifically designed by the coach with a definite purpose in mind. Indeed, with appropriate and timely intervention from the coach, this type of practice is of great help in helping players learn to make correct tactical decisions.

In addition to *tactical* decision making, players also need to learn what we might refer to as *technical* decision making. Once a player makes a tactical decision—during either practice or game play—he or she will presumably act on that decision. If, for example, the player elects to pass the ball to a teammate some 30 yards (or meters) away, then the player must instantly decide what is needed in order to deliver the pass accurately. When should the pass be released? (The player may have to hold the ball for a short period as the receiver moves into position.) What is the specific target for the pass—the player's head, chest, or feet; an area ahead of or around the player's feet; or a space for the player to move into? How can the pass being delivered elude defenders who could intercept it? How much speed should be given to the pass, and does it need backspin, sidespin, or top spin? Which part of the foot needs to contact which part of the ball, and when and how should the player arrange his or her feet, balance, and hips in order to do so?

All of these considerations must be accounted for in order to produce the necessary final contact on the ball. Sometimes the player must make the decision in an instant and, therefore, must draw on a memory bank of sensorimotor movements to complete the required action. How is this bank of movement skills created and enlarged? The answer is through experience in practice and game play. Consequently, players need to rehearse all of the motor movements that combine to allow a successful pass, and they need to do so over and over again, both in a variety of practice situations and in game play.

A game situation such as the one shown in figure 12.2 gives both player and coach the opportunity to assess the most effective action to take. In the central attacking third of the field, attacker 4 is in possession of the ball and has different options ahead of him, such as:

- Should he supply wide attacker 7 with a pass behind the fullback 3?
- Should he supply central attacker 9 with a pass between defenders 5 and 6?
- Should he supply attacker 11 with a pass to the back of the defense or should he take the ball forward and shoot at goal?

These are the options that attacker 4 may observe during a game, so how does he choose, which action does he choose and what are the considerations in making the "best" decision at that time? Given this imaginary situation in a game, what would you do if you were the player?

Factors such as the position of the goalkeeper, the distances and angles between defenders, the capability of attacker 4 to deliver what is needed by the different possible receivers, and offside rules are all part of the calculations. Only the player can make the final decision during a game but a coach can help him understand the options, the likelihood of success, and the risks involved so that he may well become a more considerate decision-maker and begin to understand the criteria for decision making when given time to do so.

The coach's duty is to help the player through thoughtful and targeted practice design and through personal assistance in understanding the biomechanics of the needed techniques and skills. A key question here is whether the coach sufficiently understands the biomechanics, ergonomics, anatomy, and physiology to assist in the player's

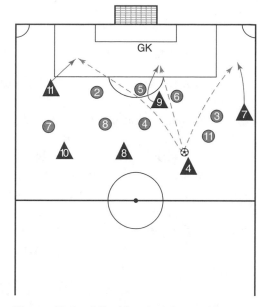

Figure 12.2 Attacking decision making.

development. Players learn to make correct tactical and technical decisions only through repeated exposure to purposeful and focused practice and play, laced with appropriate and challenging demands and accompanied by guidance from the coach as necessary. This process can be lengthy, but its rewards are substantial and fulfilling for both player and coach.

To accompany their tactical decision making, players must also develop the technical expertise in all of the necessary soccer skills in order to achieve tactical success. Decision making is best enhanced if the coach uses a variety of practice types and games. Whether this means games designed by the coach to encourage distinct aspects of play, games designed by players, or simple pickup games, players must be involved in repetitive soccer situations and be mindful of what they are seeking to develop or improve.

For example, a practice activity might be designed to help players develop ball-contact skills when unopposed, when semi-opposed, or when fully opposed in a 9v9 game. Similarly, a practice might be repetitive, or it might be varied in order to challenge players to apply spin, height, or extra speed with disguise. The point is that players should be offered a sensible mix of playing and practice experiences. Exposure to hours of concentrated, focused practice increases players' motor memory bank and helps them develop the technical and tactical decision-making skills necessary to play at the higher levels of the game.

Decision making is contextual in its essence. Playing situations may be very similar, but they are rarely identical. For example, two teams may operate with similar playing systems (for example, 4-3-3), but certain specifics—the players, the tactics, the style of play—may differ between the teams. Therefore, it is crucial that players develop a clear understanding of the principles of play, whether defending or attacking. And again, players' decisions should be grounded in a good understanding of their own attributes and capabilities. In addition, they also need to learn how to make an early preliminary decision and then follow up with either a confirmation of that decision or a change of decision.

Immersion in practice that involves making such decisions (and all types of practice involve decision making of some kind!) helps players learn to make, adjust, refine, and change decisions as necessary. Again, however, the coach's guidance and support are vital and should never be underestimated. Indeed, it is the duty of all coaches to fully explore the game in all aspects of play and to master technical and tactical variations if they are to help players make sense of the complicated game of soccer.

SOCCER INTELLIGENCE DRILL

Decision making is the essence of individual and team tactical success. The game constantly changes—almost every second that the ball is in play—and continuous decision making is the norm for both the players and the coach. Often, defenders react to the game's events whereas attackers will take initiative. Creating game scenarios that challenge the players' ability to understand and, therefore, make more correct decisions is a major function of the coach. Shown here is a simple game situation that occurs regularly in modern soccer but frequently causes confusion among defenders. The artful coach will identify and then create an abundant number of game situations that tests players' decision making both from an attacking and defending viewpoint. This is just one example of many game events that can serve as the incentive for players to think deeply about the game and their individual game.

Tactical Decision Making

Purpose

Making tactical decisions

Organization

Set up an area 35 yards from the edge of the penalty area and 30 yards in from the touchline. A goal is placed just inside the penalty area at an angle as illustrated.

Procedure

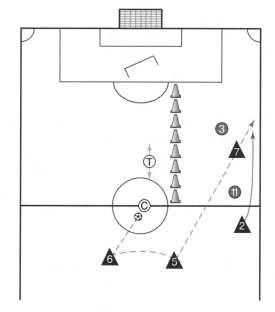

- The coach begins the practice by feeding a ball to center back 6 who is positioned approximately 15-20 yards behind the halfway line.

- Center back 6 passes to center back 5, who uses a maximum of three touches before passing the ball to either attacker 2 or 7.

- Attackers 2 and 7 combine their movements so that one of them can receive the ball from center back 5.

- Upon receiving possession, attacker 2 or 7 plays either to cross the ball into the goal from the wide area bounded by the line of cones or to move the ball into the goal from a more central area.

- Support player T can be used if needed to assist attacker 2 or 7 but cannot pass the ball into the goal. He is mobile behind the line of cones and seeks to offer support to the attackers when necessary. He should try to return passes to the attacking players within two touches if and when used by the attackers in their quest to eliminate the defenders.

- Defenders 3 and 11 should work to prevent attacker 7 from receiving the ball and turning to feed a teammate, run with the ball, or pass it into the goal. Nor should attacker 2 escape the attention of the defenders in order to receive the ball and cross it into the goal.

Coaching Points

- An early decision as to which defender takes responsibility for each attacker (2 or 7) is necessary. The defenders may also decide to mark the spaces in which 2 and 7 will move, so the decision is to either mark individual opponents or make spaces.

(continued)

Tactical Decision Making *(continued)*

- Each defender prevents their opponent from receiving the ball and exploiting the space behind them when they receive passes to the feet and turn with the ball or when they try to run to the space behind the defender to receive the ball.

- Marking opponents at the correct distance and communicating with each other will help the defenders make the appropriate decisions as they combat the movements by the two attacking players.

- Should the opponent receive the ball, the defenders must prevent the attackers from delivering the ball into the goal by pressing the player in possession, staying on his feet, and being patient until the right time to challenge for the ball arises.

The game is continuously evolving, and some key changes have been explained in the opening section of this book. The crucial factor, however, is that the game will continue to evolve, and coaches must therefore anticipate what the game will look like some 10 to 20 years from now. The skills required will be much enhanced from the present. At the highest level, it will be the norm for players to possess the capability to operate at speed and to use changes of speed while executing soccer skills. Athletic requirements will also be elevated, and decision-making capability will be increasingly tested as the game continues to speed up.

This book has been written with all of these factors in mind and geared to cover the skills and athletic areas of development that will be foundational in the future of the game. Indeed, the abilities to think and decide at speed, to act at speed, and to change direction at speed are already crucial to high-level sport in general and to soccer in particular. And they will be even more in demand in the future.

High-level sport also involves the ability to perform under pressure. The needed skills are not only technical, tactical, and athletic but also cognitive, psychological, and emotional. Top performers handle their mental and emotional states to their advantage. While this book does not address these features of performance, the authors acknowledge their importance in the development of both young and adult soccer players, and we recommend that coaches study these domains as they progress with their players toward the future game.

References

Cook, G. 2010. *Movement: Functional movement systems: Screening assessment and corrective strategies.* Aptos, CA: On Target.

Jeffreys, I. 2006. Motor learning—Applications for agility, part 1. *Strength and Conditioning Journal* 28(5):72-76.

Jeffreys, I. 2006. Motor learning—Applications for agility, part 2. *Strength and Conditioning Journal* 28(6):10-14.

Jeffreys, I. 2007. *Total soccer fitness.* Monterey, CA. Coaches Choice.

Jeffreys, I. 2008. Movement training for field sports: Soccer. *Strength and Conditioning Journal* 30(4):19-27.

Jeffreys, I. 2010. *Gamespeed: Movement training for superior sports performance.* Monterey, CA: Coaches Choice.

Jeffreys, I. 2011. A task based approach to developing reactive agility. *Strength and Conditioning Journal* 33(4):52-59.

Sheppard, J.M., and W.B. Young. 2006. *Agility literature review: Classifications, training and testing. Journal of Sports Sciences* 24: 919-932.

About the Authors

Dick Bate heads the Cardiff City FC Youth Academy and is the former director of elite coaching for the English Football Association (FA). He has coached at Leeds United FC, Notts County FC, Lincoln City FC, and Hereford United FC. He has been the technical director at Watford FC. He is a technical adviser to FIFA, soccer's world governing body. He was also the technical director of the Malaysian Football Association and the Canadian Soccer Association.

Bate is a UEFA professional license holder, FA staff coach, AFC staff coach, UEFA "A" license holder, and England youth team coach. As an athlete he played for Sheffield Wednesday, York City, and Boston United football clubs and represented the British Colleges while a student.

He has directed and conducted several UEFA Professional License courses and more than 40 UEFA "A" license courses and, together with S. Subramaniam, devised and instigated the Coach Education Programme throughout Asia for the Asian Football Confederation. He received the Lifetime Achievement Coaching Award from the English Football Association.

Bate is in demand as a speaker and presenter. In a presentation to the National Soccer Coaches Association of America titled "Soccer 2020: The Future of the World's Game," Dick described how soccer has evolved into a game that rewards players who can master speed and agility skills under match pressure—one-touch passing and receiving, retaining and regaining possession, fakes and feints, and quick changes in direction.

Ian Jeffreys is one of the most respected strength and conditioning coaches in the United Kingdom and a world-renowned authority on speed and agility development. He is a reader and director of strength and conditioning at the University of South Wales. He is also the proprietor and performance director of All-Pro Performance based in Brecon, Wales. Ian has been a member of the National Strength and Conditioning Association (NSCA) since 1989. He is a registered strength and conditioning

coach, certified strength and conditioning specialist (CSCS), and certified personal trainer (NSCA-CPT) with the NSCA and has been recertified with distinction (*D) in all categories. He was the NSCA's High School Professional of the Year in 2006, the first time the award had ever been presented to a coach working outside the United States. In July 2009, Ian was awarded a fellowship by the NSCA for his outstanding contributions to the industry. He is an accredited strength and conditioning coach with the United Kingdom Strength and Conditioning Association (UKSCA) and was on the board of directors of the association from its founding in 2004 until 2013.

Ian has authored 4 books, 10 book chapters, and numerous strength and conditioning articles that have been featured in leading international journals. He also edited the NSCA book *Developing Speed* (Human Kinetics, 2013).

Ian has worked with numerous clubs and sport organizations around the world. He is a sought-after conference presenter and has given keynote presentations and hosted performance workshops at several worldwide conferences, including the NSCA Sport-Specific and European Conferences and the Australian Strength and Conditioning Conference.